For permissions or inquiries:
**author.isla.quinn@gmail.com**

First Edition: 2025
Cover design and layout by Isla Quinn
Printed and published in Canada.

# Table of Contents

# Part I: Foundations of Astrology

## Chapter 1: What Is Astrology?

*Or: Why Your Ex Being a Scorpio Isn't the Whole Story*

### Let's Begin With the Basics (But Not the Boring Kind)

Astrology. You've probably heard people talk about it with wildly different energy.

There's the enthusiastic friend who swears Mercury retrograde ruined her week. The skeptic who says, "There's no way billions of people can be divided into 12 types." And then there's you—curious, maybe intrigued, looking for something deeper than vague horoscopes and meme astrology. You want to feel seen, understood, maybe even validated for that emotional reaction you had last Thursday at 3:17 p.m. when you swore the universe was trying to send you a sign.

Let me reassure you: astrology is not about putting you in a box. It's about giving you the keys to the box you already live in—and helping you redecorate it with intention. Think of it like IKEA instructions for your soul's growth, minus the hex key and existential dread. You get to build your own understanding of yourself, one planetary insight at a time.

Astrology is the symbolic language of the sky. It interprets planetary movements and their placements at the time of your birth to reveal patterns about your personality, emotional makeup, life challenges, strengths, and even the kinds of energies you'll meet in love, career, and growth. It doesn't control you—it reflects you. The same way a weather report doesn't make it rain, astrology doesn't make you feel things—but it tells you when you might want to bring an umbrella for your mood. Or maybe an emotional raincoat. Possibly both.

### The Origins of Astrology: This Isn't Just Trendy, It's Ancient

Astrology is old. Like, *before TikTok, before WiFi, before soap* old.

Its roots go back over 4,000 years to the Babylonians, who first tracked celestial movements to predict seasonal changes and major events. Later, ancient Egyptians aligned astrology with their gods. The Greeks (hi, Ptolemy!) formalized it, giving us the Western zodiac we know today. Meanwhile, Vedic astrology in India was quietly slaying the cosmic game with a whole other system.

All of these ancient civilizations looked up and saw meaning in the sky:

**Babylonian Astrology**: The Babylonians were the original stargazers. They mapped the ecliptic (the Sun's path through the sky), divided it into 12 equal parts, and basically gave us the zodiac. They used astrology for kings and wars, not love and brunch plans—but we still owe them big time.

**Egyptian Astrology**: The Egyptians merged astronomy and mysticism, assigning gods and goddesses to constellations and stars. Their decans (10-degree segments of the zodiac) influenced how we time planetary strength.

**Vedic Astrology (Jyotish)**: Rooted in India, this sidereal system focuses on karma, dharma, and precision. It's more predictive and spiritually structured than Western astrology, with planetary periods (called *dashas*) that map out the big chapters of your life.

**Hellenistic Astrology**: The Greeks brought geometry, logic, and a flair for storytelling. With philosophers like Ptolemy, they turned astrology into a system of houses, aspects, and planetary dignities that still form the backbone of Western astrology.

Your birth chart is essentially the heirloom of this rich, multicultural legacy. It's part math, part myth, part therapy, and part cosmic art.

### Astrology and Astronomy: Starry Siblings With Very Different Jobs

Long ago, astrology and astronomy were the same thing. The study of stars and planets served both spiritual and scientific purposes. Even famous thinkers like Galileo and Kepler dabbled in both.

Over time, astronomy became the math-and-science nerd: calculating orbits, launching satellites, discovering galaxies. Astrology took the path of the mystic poet, saying, "Sure, that's cool… but what does it *mean* when Mars is in Cancer?"

| **Astronomy** | **Astrology** |
|---|---|
| Studies celestial bodies using physics and math | Interprets the symbolic meaning of those celestial bodies |
| Objective, measurable data | Subjective, archetypal insight |

| | |
|---|---|
| Think: telescopes, space probes | Think: natal charts, moon journals |

If astronomy is Google Maps, astrology is the playlist you make for the trip. Both helpful. Just different vibes. And your vibes? Worth tracking.

### The Birth Chart: Your Cosmic Blueprint

Imagine the universe as your personal paparazzi, snapping a photo of the sky the moment you were born. That cosmic selfie is your natal chart. It's a 360-degree wheel of the sky, centered on you (yes, you), capturing the planetary lineup at your birth. This chart is your cosmic DNA—it explains why you're passionate, introspective, allergic to small talk, and obsessed with your Spotify "On Repeat" playlist.

This chart is deeply personal. Even if someone was born the same day as you, just minutes apart, their chart could look totally different. Why? Because astrology isn't just date-based—it's time- and location-sensitive too. Basically, it's the most accurate time-stamped receipt you'll ever get. And unlike your last Amazon order, this one actually helps you understand yourself.

### Astrology Is Like... A Symphony (or a Soup, or a Sitcom)

Here's one way to think about it:

**The planets** are the actors in your personal story. They represent different parts of you—your identity, emotions, drive, love style, communication habits, and more. Each one is a facet of you showing up to play its role.

**The signs** are the costumes those actors wear. They show how your inner energies express themselves. Are you bold like Aries, nurturing like Cancer, or analytical like Virgo? These signs flavor the way you show up in the world.

**The houses** are the stage settings. They represent where the action happens in your life—love, career, friendships, home, or personal growth. Each house shows where a particular part of you is most active or challenged.

**The aspects** (we'll get to those later) are the relationships between the actors. Do parts of you get along and support each other? Or do they argue like your inner perfectionist and your inner free spirit trying to plan a vacation together? Sometimes your internal dynamics are a love triangle. Sometimes they're a group chat gone passive-aggressive.

Altogether, your chart is like watching a sitcom written about you, starring you, and occasionally being directed by you (when the planets aren't running wild).

Or, if you're more of a foodie: Think of the Sun sign as the main ingredient in your personality stew. But your Moon sign is the secret spice—your inner flavor. The Ascendant (or Rising sign) is the presentation—it's how the dish is plated and what others see first. You wouldn't describe a meal based on one ingredient, would you? That's why the "What's your sign?" question only scratches the surface. You are way more deliciously complex than that.

### You Are Not Just Your Sun Sign

Let me say it louder for the people in the back: You are not just your Sun sign.

Yes, your Sun sign matters. It's your essence, your solar glow, your personality's anchor.

But there's also:

- **Your Moon sign** (your emotional HQ, where you go to cry or eat cheese in private)
- **Your Rising sign** (your cosmic outfit, your vibe, the reason people always say you look like you have your life together)
- **Your Venus** (how you flirt, love, and maybe ghost)
- **Your Mars** (how you pursue goals, start fights, or win pillow talk)
- **Your Mercury** (how you think, text, and possibly overanalyze)

And let's not forget:

2. **Saturn**: the tough-love teacher
3. **Jupiter**: your cosmic hype squad
4. **Uranus**: the chaos agent
5. **Neptune**: the daydreamer
6. **Pluto**: the deep-sea diver of your psyche

Basically, your chart is an entire cast of characters—and you're both the main character and the director. Dramatic? Yes. Accurate? Also yes.

### Types of Astrology: A Flavor for Every Mood

Astrology isn't just about reading your birth chart and calling it a day. There are different branches—like Hogwarts houses, but celestial. Here are a few core types you'll hear about (and probably want to dabble in):

**Natal Astrology**: This is your origin story. Your natal chart, cast for the exact time and place you were born, reveals your personality, desires, fears, and fate flavor. It's the most foundational type and where we start in this book.

**Transit Astrology**: The planets never stop moving. Transit astrology looks at how the current sky is interacting with your natal chart. That sudden urge to change your life during eclipse season? Yeah. That's probably Uranus throwing shade at your Moon.

**Synastry Astrology**: This is compatibility astrology. It compares two birth charts to see how the energies mesh. It's not just for romantic partners—it works for friends, family, and even coworkers (yes, Karen's Mars might actually square your Saturn).

**Horary Astrology**: You ask a question ("Where are my AirPods?" or "Should I take this job?"), and the astrologer casts a chart for the moment the question is asked. Surprisingly specific and often freaky accurate.

**Electional Astrology**: Need to schedule something important—like a wedding, a business launch, or a breakup? Electional astrology helps pick the best time, based on the sky's mood. It's celestial timing 101.

There are other advanced forms (progressions, solar arcs, draconic charts…), but we'll ease into those later. For now, just know astrology is way more than a BuzzFeed quiz—it's a full-blown system of cosmic insight.

### Astrology Is Not…

- A religion (you can be Christian, Buddhist, agnostic, or a skeptical yoga-loving coffee drinker and still vibe with astrology)

- An excuse for bad behavior ("Sorry I ghosted you, Mercury made me do it!" is still not cool)
- About changing your fate (it's about understanding your patterns)
- Just horoscopes (though they can be fun and sometimes eerily accurate)

**Why Use Astrology? (Besides Winning at Meme Battles)**

Astrology helps you:

- Understand your emotional needs
- Communicate better
- Time things wisely (Saturn return wedding, anyone?)
- Work through karmic patterns
- Embrace your full complexity

It's self-awareness, but make it cosmic. Therapy with sparkles. A roadmap with plot twists and snack breaks. Astrology gives you a language to articulate who you are, where you're going, and why certain things feel so damn familiar.

**Is It Real Though?**

Define *real*. Do you mean scientifically measurable? No. But can it change how you see yourself and others? 100% yes. Astrology works not because it dictates your life, but because it reflects your patterns.

If you've ever read your chart and thought, "How is this so accurate?"—welcome to the club. If you haven't yet—buckle up.

**So Why This Book?**

Because astrology shouldn't feel intimidating. You don't need a PhD in symbolic geometry to understand yourself better. You just need a little curiosity and a willingness to look up (and in). This book is for you—the real, messy, stardust-coated you—who's ready to decode the vibes and understand what makes you tick, love, rage, and evolve.

**Astrology Is an Invitation**

Astrology won't fix your life. But it will help you see it—with more compassion, curiosity, and a touch of stardust.

It's not a rulebook. It's a mirror. A map. A cosmic mixtape reminding you that you're made of starlight and stumbles, and that both are allowed.

So go ahead: read your chart. Laugh at the chaos. Cry at the Moon. Wonder why Saturn is roasting your love life. It's all part of the show.

**Welcome to the stars. Let's get to know you.**

## Chapter 2: The Zodiac Wheel

*Meet the Zodiac Signs – Your Cosmic Reality Show Cast*

### Welcome to Your Star-Studded Life

So you're ready to meet your astrological cast. Think of the zodiac signs as the stars of your personal cosmic reality show. Each sign brings its own flavor, drama, charm, quirks, and yes—occasional meltdown. They're not here to label you; they're here to help you understand your strengths, challenges, and hidden superpowers.

Your natal chart is filled with these archetypes. Even if you know your Sun sign, remember: every planet in your chart wears one of these cosmic costumes, influencing your personality in unique ways. Grab your popcorn—here's the lineup!

### The 12 Zodiac Signs

#### Aries (March 21 - April 19): The Trailblazing Influencer

Aries is the first sign of the zodiac—and it acts like it. Ruled by Mars, Aries is all about new beginnings, fierce independence, and the energy of a thousand triple espressos. Aries is your internal hype-person who yells "Do it!" before your inner voice can talk you out of it.

In your chart, Aries shows where you're bold, assertive, and action-oriented—but also where you may be impulsive or combative. If your Mars is in Aries, for example, you probably charge headfirst into challenges. If your Moon's in Aries, you might emotionally react before you've even realized why.

At their best, Aries placements inspire courage, leadership, and raw authenticity. At their worst? Think impatient, reckless, and possibly yelling in all caps.

Aries energy says: Don't wait for permission. Start now. Learn through action. Just maybe... wear a helmet.

#### Taurus (April 20 - May 20): The Sensual Comfort-Seeker

Taurus is fixed earth, and it's the slow-burning, sensual anchor of the zodiac. Ruled by Venus, Taurus energy is all about beauty, touch, taste, and security. It's that vibe that makes you want to light candles, wear soft clothes, and eat chocolate you don't have to share.

Taurus teaches you to slow down and be present. If Taurus shows up strongly in your chart, you likely crave stability, consistency, and luxurious comfort—even if it's a high-thread-count blanket and a perfectly curated Spotify playlist. Taurus is that friend who remembers your snack preferences and always pays for quality over quantity.

Downside? Taurus can be stubborn. Like "I'd rather suffer silently than change" stubborn. But the lesson? Sometimes being grounded and loyal to your values is a strength. And other times, you've gotta roll with the changes.

**Gemini (May 21 - June 20): The Quick-Witted Communicator**

Ruled by Mercury, Gemini is the buzzing bee of the zodiac. Curious, talkative, witty, and adaptable, Gemini energy is always gathering information, telling stories, and thinking five thoughts at once.

Gemini placements in your chart show where you crave stimulation and connection. Mercury in Gemini loves wordplay and clever comebacks. Venus in Gemini? Flirtatious texts, witty banter, and ghosting for intellectual boredom.

When you channel Gemini's high road, you're articulate, curious, and engaging. On the flip side? Scattered, indecisive, and distracted by shiny ideas. But hey, who doesn't want a mental kaleidoscope once in a while?

Gemini says: Ask questions. Stay curious. Learn everything. Then tell everyone.

**Cancer (June 21 - July 22): The Nurturing Empath**

Cancer is ruled by the Moon, and its energy is soft, emotional, and deeply maternal. Cancer is the zodiac's nurturer—it remembers your allergies, holds space for your feelings, and probably has extra snacks in its bag.

Cancer placements reveal your emotional style and where you tend to create safe spaces. With your Moon in Cancer, your emotional world is tidal—changing, flowing, but always deep. Venus in Cancer? You love through nurturing, nostalgia, and intuitive understanding.

But don't mistake tenderness for weakness. Cancer's symbol is the crab for a reason. There's a soft inside and a protective shell. If hurt, Cancer retreats—but never forgets. Its memory is photographic, especially when it comes to emotional wounds.

Cancer says: Feel fully. Protect fiercely. Love deeply.

**Leo (July 23 - August 22): The Charismatic Performer**

Leo, ruled by the Sun, is the zodiac's radiant heart. Think charisma, confidence, creativity—and occasionally, a flair for the dramatic. Leo placements bring warmth, joy, and a deep need to be seen and appreciated.

If your Sun is in Leo, you're born to shine. Leo Moon? You need recognition and heartfelt affection to feel emotionally secure. Mars in Leo? You approach challenges with pride and passion.

Leo teaches us to lead with our hearts and honor our inner royalty. But too much Leo can lead to ego battles, attention-seeking, or "main character syndrome." Leo's growth edge is learning to share the stage, uplift others, and lead from love—not from the need for applause.

Leo says: Celebrate your light. Lift others up with it.

**Virgo (August 23 - September 22): The Detail-Oriented Editor**

Virgo, Mercury's earthy child, is precise, practical, and purpose-driven. It's the sign of refinement, rituals, and service. Virgo sees what needs fixing—and immediately makes a to-do list.

Virgo placements bring analytical gifts, a keen eye, and a deep desire to be useful. A Virgo Sun person might strive for self-improvement and efficiency. Moon in Virgo? You find emotional comfort in order and competence. Mercury in Virgo? Laser-focused thinking and excellent editing skills.

At its highest, Virgo heals through precision. But in shadow, it can become overly critical—of self and others—and get stuck trying to fix what was never broken.

Virgo says: Improve gently. Serve with love. Perfection isn't required—presence is.

**Libra (September 23 - October 22): The Diplomatic Peacemaker**

Libra is ruled by Venus and brings grace, social charm, and a deep love of harmony. It's the sign of relationships, beauty, justice, and aesthetic obsession. Libra placements know how to keep the peace—and look good doing it.

Libra in your chart reveals how you relate to others. Sun in Libra? You're a natural diplomat. Moon in Libra? Emotional equilibrium is key. Venus in Libra? You love love—and also a well-set dinner table with matching candles.

But Libra's desire for peace can lead to people-pleasing or decision paralysis. Its lesson? True harmony requires honesty—and sometimes, temporary discomfort. Not all things pretty are peaceful underneath.

Libra says: Seek balance. Speak truth with kindness. Choose love over likes.

**Scorpio (October 23 - November 21): The Intense Investigator**

Scorpio, co-ruled by Pluto and Mars, dives deep. Its waters run dark, powerful, and transformative. This is the energy of psychological excavation, soul-merging intimacy, and ultimate rebirth.

Scorpio placements bring intensity wherever they land. Scorpio Sun? You embody depth, resilience, and emotional x-ray vision. Moon in Scorpio? You *feel* everything and trust almost no one until proven otherwise. Mars in Scorpio? Laser focus and magnetic ambition.

Scorpio teaches that power comes through vulnerability and that transformation requires letting go. But when unbalanced, Scorpio can become possessive, jealous, or addicted to emotional control.

Scorpio says: Go deep. Burn away what no longer serves. Rebirth is your superpower.

**Sagittarius (November 22 - December 21): The Adventurous Explorer**

Ruled by Jupiter, Sagittarius is wild, wise, and wonderfully unfiltered. It's the seeker, teacher, wanderer, and philosopher. Sagittarius placements light up the part of your chart that wants to grow, expand, and learn forever.

Sun in Sag? You're fueled by freedom, truth, and long walks into the unknown. Moon in Sag? Emotional security comes from experiences and a sense of possibility. Mercury in Sag? Blunt honesty, big ideas, and a loud internal narrator.

Sagittarius teaches you to question assumptions, embrace diversity, and laugh in the face of monotony. But don't let optimism become avoidance—or dogma.

Sagittarius says: Chase meaning. Pack light. And maybe check your facts before ranting.

### Capricorn (December 22 - January 19): The Ambitious Achiever

Capricorn, ruled by Saturn, is the adult in the zodiac room. It's focused, determined, and loyal to long-term goals. Capricorn placements show where you're disciplined, competent, and deeply invested in mastery.

Sun in Capricorn? You respect structure, timelines, and slow-building success. Moon in Capricorn? You protect your feelings behind work ethic and ambition. Mars in Capricorn? You achieve like a boss—grinding today for tomorrow's legacy.

Capricorn teaches us to climb our personal mountains with resilience and wisdom. But beware of burnout and emotional detachment. You're not your productivity. Rest is revolutionary.

Capricorn says: Build slowly. Think long-term. Keep your integrity.

### Aquarius (January 20 - February 18): The Innovative Rebel

Aquarius, ruled by Uranus and Saturn, is the zodiac's brilliant oddball. It values freedom, vision, and collective evolution. Aquarius placements highlight where you break molds, think ahead, and crave community.

Sun in Aquarius? You're unique, intelligent, and probably allergic to conformity. Moon in Aquarius? You need emotional autonomy and intellectual stimulation. Mercury in Aquarius? Hello, futuristic thinker.

Aquarius teaches that individuality and humanity are not opposites. Its challenge? Balancing the head and the heart—don't forget to feel while you fight for change.

Aquarius says: Be original. Be weird. Be for the people.

**Pisces (February 19 - March 20): The Dreamy Mystic**

Pisces, ruled by Neptune, is the sign of surrender, soul, and infinite creativity. It blurs boundaries between self and other, waking life and dream. Pisces placements bring sensitivity, intuition, and imagination.

Sun in Pisces? You're a feeler, healer, and sometimes a space cadet (with love). Moon in Pisces? You soak up vibes like a sponge. Venus in Pisces? Romance meets fantasy. You're in love with love.

Pisces teaches compassion and connection beyond logic. Its pitfalls? Escapism, martyrdom, or losing your identity in others. Boundaries are spiritual armor.

Pisces says: Feel everything. Dream big. Ground the magic.

**The Elements: Fire, Earth, Air, Water**

Astrology is made of more than stars—it's made of elements. Each sign belongs to one of four elements, which flavor how its energy expresses. These four elemental forces—Fire, Earth, Air, and Water—aren't just symbolic. They define the energetic temperament of each sign and provide the emotional seasoning behind the zodiac's personality stew.

| Element | Signs | Superpowers | Shadow Side |
|---|---|---|---|
| Fire | Aries, Leo, Sagittarius | Passion, vitality, leadership | Impulsiveness, anger, drama |
| Earth | Taurus, Virgo, Capricorn | Practicality, loyalty, stability | Rigidity, materialism, fear of change |

| | | | |
|---|---|---|---|
| Air | Gemini, Libra, Aquarius | Intellect, communication, ideas | Detachment, overthinking, aloofness |
| Water | Cancer, Scorpio, Pisces | Emotion, empathy, intuition | Moodiness, escapism, codependency |

You don't need to be "a fire sign" to feel fiery, or "a water sign" to feel waves of emotion. You've got all four elements operating in your chart somewhere. But understanding what each one *means*? That's when astrology starts singing in surround sound.

### Fire Signs: Aries, Leo, Sagittarius

Fire signs are the sparks, the flame-throwers, the "YES let's do it" crew. They bring action, heat, charisma, and confidence. They're passionate, instinctive, and don't wait for a group vote before jumping into life.

When fire signs are balanced, they light up the room with joy, ambition, and inspiration. They teach us to go after what we want without apology. But when fire gets too wild? It burns out, burns bridges, or just burns everyone out.

- **High vibe**: Courage, creativity, vitality
- **Low vibe**: Impatience, drama, overconfidence

Fire asks: What lights you up—and are you feeding that flame?

### Earth Signs: Taurus, Virgo, Capricorn

Earth signs are the roots, the builders, the grown-ups of the zodiac. They thrive on reliability, structure, and grounded action. They value results, loyalty, and the satisfaction of a job well done.

Earth reminds us to slow down, get practical, and pay our bills (ugh, fine). But too much earth? You might dig in your heels, resist change, or forget there's more to life than your to-do list.

7. **High vibe**: Stability, responsibility, sensuality
8. **Low vibe**: Stubbornness, materialism, rigidity

Earth asks: What keeps you grounded—and is it helping you grow?

### Air Signs: Gemini, Libra, Aquarius

Air signs are the idea-makers, the social butterflies, and the eternal students. They live in their heads, but not in a bad way—they're wired for analysis, connection, and problem-solving.

When air signs are elevated, they're brilliant communicators and innovative thinkers. But left unchecked, air can float too far off the ground—getting stuck in theory or lost in their own thoughts.

- **High vibe**: Clarity, curiosity, intelligence
- **Low vibe**: Overthinking, detachment, flakiness

Air asks: What thoughts are filling your lungs—and are they fresh or recycled?

### Water Signs: Cancer, Scorpio, Pisces

Water signs are the feelers, the empaths, and the emotional alchemists. They move through life in waves—feeling deeply, intuiting everything, and absorbing emotions like human sponges.

Balanced water is soothing, creative, and deeply connected. But too much? Hello, emotional overwhelm, codependency, and mysterious disappearing acts.

- **High vibe**: Compassion, intuition, emotional depth
- **Low vibe**: Moody, escapist, hypersensitive

Water asks: Where do your feelings flow—and what needs cleansing?

### Modalities: Cardinal, Fixed, Mutable

If the elements describe your *style*, the modalities describe your *strategy, m*odalities explain *how* signs take action and respond to life.

The modality of a sign reveals how it initiates, sustains, or adapts to life's movement.

| **Modality** | **Signs** | **Energy Style** | **Keyword** |
|---|---|---|---|
| Cardinal | Aries, Cancer, Libra, Capricorn | Initiating, ambitious, leading | Start |
| Fixed | Taurus, Leo, Scorpio, Aquarius | Stable, consistent, enduring | Sustain |
| Mutable | Gemini, Virgo, Sagittarius, Pisces | Adaptive, flexible, changing | Transition |

Modalities combined with elements give each sign its distinct personality. For example:

- Leo = Fixed Fire → enduring charisma
- Virgo = Mutable Earth → flexible practicality
- Capricorn = Cardinal Earth → ambitious builder

**Cardinal Signs: Aries, Cancer, Libra, Capricorn**

Cardinal signs are the starters. They launch seasons and initiate energy. They have a proactive spirit and often take the lead—even when no one asked them to.

These signs are visionary, motivated, and great at taking the first step. But follow-through? That's another story. They need support systems to bring their bold ideas to the finish line.

- **High vibe**: Leadership, initiative, momentum
- **Low vibe**: Bossy, scattered, short attention span

Cardinal asks: What are you starting—and are you building it with purpose?

**Fixed Signs: Taurus, Leo, Scorpio, Aquarius**

Fixed signs are the anchors. They stabilize, preserve, and protect. Once they're on a path, they stick with it like Velcro on purpose.

They're reliable and committed, often embodying tenacity and loyalty. But beware their resistance to change—once fixed signs dig in, they may refuse to budge.

- **High vibe**: Determination, loyalty, depth
- **Low vibe**: Stubbornness, inflexibility, obsession

Fixed asks: What are you committed to—and is it still serving your evolution?

### Mutable Signs: Gemini, Virgo, Sagittarius, Pisces

Mutable signs are the adapters. They're the ones who bend with the wind and read the room like pros. They mark the end of seasons and are always prepping for the next chapter.

These signs are flexible, versatile, and open-minded. But too much mutability can lead to anxiety, identity shifts, or indecisiveness. They're great at flowing—but need grounding to thrive.

- **High vibe**: Flexibility, adaptability, openness
- **Low vibe**: Flaky, unfocused, overly impressionable

Mutable asks: How do you respond to change—and are you transforming or escaping?

### How Signs Express Themselves

Every sign has a *spectrum* of expression. One end is the evolved, empowered version of the sign. The other? Let's just say... a work in progress.

Understanding this helps you embrace the high road—and catch yourself when you're veering off it.

### A Few Deep-Dive Examples:

#### Aries

- Evolved: Bold, brave, initiator, warrior with heart
- Unevolved: Impulsive, aggressive, tantrum-prone toddler with a sword

**Taurus**

- Evolved: Loyal, grounded, calm, pleasure-positive
- Unevolved: Lazy, possessive, allergic to change

**Gemini**

- Evolved: Curious, witty, a natural communicator
- Unevolved: Inconsistent, two-faced, talking with zero listening

**Cancer**

- Evolved: Empathic, nurturing, deeply intuitive
- Unevolved: Manipulative, emotionally moody, mothering the unwilling

**Leo**

- Evolved: Inspiring, generous, warm-hearted
- Unevolved: Self-absorbed, bossy, melodramatic

**Virgo**

- Evolved: Humble, service-oriented, sharp as hell
- Unevolved: Judgy, anxious, obsessing over invisible flaws

**Libra**

- Evolved: Balanced, diplomatic, aesthetically blessed
- Unevolved: Indecisive, fake-nice, allergic to confrontation

**Scorpio**

- Evolved: Deep, transformative, loyal to the soul
- Unevolved: Possessive, secretive, emotionally vindictive

**Sagittarius**

- Evolved: Wise, free-spirited, eternally curious
- Unevolved: Preachy, tactless, commitment-phobic

**Capricorn**

- Evolved: Wise leader, disciplined, legacy-builder
- Unevolved: Cold, status-obsessed, emotionally constipated

**Aquarius**

- Evolved: Visionary, humanitarian, inclusive
- Unevolved: Detached, contrarian, rebel without a pause

**Pisces**

- Evolved: Mystical, compassionate, divinely creative
- Unevolved: Escapist, flaky, forever lost in their feels

Signs don't define your destiny. They describe your *tools*. It's how you use them that tells your story.

### You Contain All 12 Signs

Even if you don't have any planets in Pisces, or you swear up and down you "don't vibe with Scorpios," guess what? You've got every sign in your chart—each one rules a house, a realm of life.

So yes, you *do* have a little Leo flair and some Virgo anxiety. You're a blend, a mosaic, a walking zodiac remix. That's the magic.

# Chapter 3: The Houses

*Twelve Astrological Houses, Twelve Life Arenas*

## What Are Houses, Anyway?

Imagine the sky as a giant wheel divided into twelve slices. Each slice, or "house," represents a different area of your life. While the zodiac signs describe how you experience life, the houses show **where** in your life those experiences play out. They're like the set locations for your cosmic movie: home, work, relationships, inner life — it's all covered.

Your natal chart is essentially a snapshot of the sky the moment you were born, and the houses are arranged according to your exact birth time and location. They rotate throughout the day, meaning two people born on the same date but at different times can have completely different house placements — and thus, very different life focuses. Think of it like the astrological version of "location, location, location." You might be a Cancer Sun like your cousin Janet, but if her Sun falls in the 10th house and yours is in the 4th? Whole different life story, babe.

Astrological houses are one of the most grounded parts of your chart — they deal with real-life stuff: your money, your career, your friends, your Netflix-alone time. Some astrologers even say the houses matter more than the signs themselves, because they show where the cosmic action actually plays out.

In this chapter, we'll walk through all twelve houses, one by one, showing what each governs, how to interpret planets within them, and what it means when a house is empty (spoiler: it's not bad!). You'll learn how each house tells part of your story — from your early upbringing to your career path to your wildest hopes and dreams.

## The Twelve Houses

### 1st House: The House of Self

**Keywords:** Identity, physical appearance, self-image, first impressions

This is the house of YOU — your personality, energy, physical body, and how others perceive you at first glance. It's the red carpet entrance to your cosmic essence.

The sign on the cusp of your 1st house is your **Ascendant** or **Rising sign** — and it colors how you move through life. Are you an Aries Rising, charging forward with fire in your eyes? Or a Libra Rising, exuding charm and balance like your life is an Instagram filter?

Planets in the 1st house make a huge impact. The Sun here gives natural confidence. The Moon? Emotional expression is front and center. Mars? Bold, driven, possibly impatient. Venus? Beauty, grace, and serious selfie game.

This house also governs your early conditioning — how you learned to present yourself, how you respond to the world, and how the world responds to you. It's like your astrological name tag.

**Reflection questions:** How do I instinctively show up? What is my vibe when I walk into a room? What "mask" do I wear without realizing it?

### 2nd House: The House of Value

**Keywords:** Money, possessions, self-worth, resources

Let's talk worth. The 2nd house rules what you own, what you value, and how you value yourself. It's the house of material reality and internal security.

On a literal level, this house governs income, finances, savings, shopping habits, and your relationship with money. Do you splurge when you're sad? Save like a squirrel in winter? The sign on your 2nd house cusp, and any planets there, will tell you how you earn and what makes you feel rich — emotionally and financially.

More symbolically, it's about **self-worth**. How confident are you in your own value? Do you believe you deserve love, success, support? This house shows whether you build your self-esteem from the inside or seek it through external validation.

- **Saturn** here might delay financial success or cause scarcity beliefs.
- **Jupiter** may bring abundance — but you'll need to manage excess.
- **Venus** often brings ease with money, but maybe a taste for luxury.

**Ask yourself:** What do I believe I'm worth? Do my spending habits align with my values? Where do I overgive or undervalue myself?

**3rd House: The House of Communication**
**Keywords:** Thought, speech, writing, siblings, short travel

This house governs your mind — not the dreamy subconscious, but your **everyday thinking**. It reveals how you learn, how you teach, how you speak, text, post, joke, gossip, and even how you talk to yourself.

It also rules **siblings**, your immediate environment, short trips (like weekend getaways), and neighbors. This is the "what's going on in your neighborhood" house — the familiar, local world around you.

Planets here shape your communication style:

9. **Mercury** here? You're chatty, curious, sharp-witted.
10. **Saturn**? You speak with caution — or authority.
11. **Neptune**? You're poetic… or sometimes unclear.

This house can also show social anxiety or ease, communication blocks, or the gift of gab. It tells you whether you prefer deep convos, snappy tweets, or writing your thoughts in journals you never show anyone.

**Reflection:** How do I process information? How do I communicate under stress? Do I speak to connect — or to perform?

**4th House: The House of Home and Roots**
**Keywords:** Home, family, ancestry, emotional foundation

This house sits at the very bottom of the chart — your foundation. It rules your **home base**, both literal and emotional. It speaks to your childhood, ancestry, inner sanctuary, and your relationship to safety and comfort.

The 4th house cusp is called the **IC** (Imum Coeli), Latin for "bottom of the sky." It's where we retreat, protect, and regenerate. It can represent the parent who shaped your inner world (often the mother, but not always).

Planets here show what "home" means to you:

- **Moon** here = deep attachment to home, family, and emotional memories.
- **Mars** = possible family conflict or strong drive to protect your space.

- **Pluto** = ancestral wounds, intense transformation through family.

An empty 4th house doesn't mean you don't care about home. It just means that other houses might hold more weight in your chart.

**Deep dive:** What was home like for me growing up? What family patterns am I repeating or healing? What does emotional security feel like?

**5th House: The House of Pleasure**
**Keywords:** Creativity, romance, children, joy, performance

Welcome to your inner stage. This house rules fun, flirting, hobbies, dating, art, and anything you create for the sheer joy of it. This is where your inner child comes out to play.

It's also associated with **children** — literal (if you have them), or metaphorical (creative projects, personal passions, anything you birth into the world).

Planets in the 5th house amplify your creative expression:

- **Sun** = natural performer, playful and magnetic
- **Saturn** = delayed joy, but serious creative mastery
- **Uranus** = unusual hobbies or avant-garde artistry

This house also gives clues about your **romantic style** before commitment. Flings, flirtations, and summer love live here.

**Ask yourself:** Where do I feel most alive? Do I allow myself to play without productivity? What lights me up and makes me glow?

**6th House: The House of Health and Service**
**Keywords:** Wellness, work, routines, responsibility, humility

This is the house of **daily devotion** — not flashy or dramatic, but sacred all the same. It rules your health, job duties, rituals, routines, pets (yes!), and how you show up to serve others.

Where the 10th house is career legacy, the 6th is your **work-life reality** — the behind-the-scenes grind. It governs your relationship to responsibility, self-care, and humble service.

- **Planets here** can indicate chronic health patterns, OCD tendencies, love of order, or burnout risk.
- **Mercury** here thrives on organized thinking.
- **Neptune** might blur boundaries around rest or enable self-sacrifice.

This house asks: Are your habits supporting you or draining you?

**Reflection:** How do I treat my body? How do I handle responsibility? Am I honoring both effort and rest?

### 7th House: The House of Relationships

**Keywords:** Partnership, marriage, contracts, mirroring, balance

This house is where you meet the mirror. The 7th governs serious one-on-one relationships: marriages, business partners, even enemies (yup — open enemies live here).

It also reflects what you **project** onto others — traits you don't own in yourself yet.

- **Venus** here = loves harmony, devoted partner
- **Mars** = passionate partnerships, but potential power struggles
- **Saturn** = slow-to-commit, but loyal once there

Look to the sign on the cusp for insight into your relationship patterns. It tells you what kind of person balances or complements you.

**Ask:** What traits do I admire (or reject) in others? What does commitment mean to me? Do I fear or crave deep partnership?

### 8th House: The House of Transformation

**Keywords:** Death, rebirth, intimacy, power, shared assets

Welcome to the deep end. The 8th house is about merging — financially, emotionally, sexually, spiritually. It governs taboo topics, shadow work, trauma healing, and transformation.

This house rules what's shared — inheritances, joint bank accounts, sexuality, and soul-deep bonding. It's also the house of death — literal or symbolic — and rebirth.

- **Pluto** here? You're a phoenix: burned, but rising.
- **Venus**? You may love deeply and transform through connection.
- **Saturn**? Intimacy might come with boundaries, trust issues, or karmic lessons.

It's also your **psychological basement** — what you keep locked away until life forces you to open it.

**Inquire:** Where am I asked to let go? What part of me seeks rebirth? How do I share power and vulnerability?

**9th House: The House of Expansion**
**Keywords:** Philosophy, higher learning, publishing, belief systems

This house is about the **big picture**. While the 3rd house is your daily mental chatter, the 9th is about beliefs, higher education, travel, spirituality, and the quest for meaning.

It rules anything that expands your worldview: study abroad, a book that changed your life, religious revelations, or a TED Talk that made you cry in public.

- **Jupiter** here loves growth, teaching, travel
- **Saturn** can bring discipline in studies, but also dogma
- **Neptune** may blur boundaries between truth and fantasy

This house asks you to define your inner compass and seek answers that connect you to something greater.

**Ask yourself:** What do I believe about life and purpose? What truths have I outgrown? Where am I called to teach or travel?

**10th House: The House of Career and Public Life**
**Keywords:** Reputation, goals, authority, public roles

The 10th is your **legacy** house. It governs ambition, success, visibility, leadership, and your impact on the world. The cusp of this house is the **Midheaven** or **MC**, your public persona and career trajectory.

This isn't just your job — it's what you're *known for.* It's your mission, your goals, your status, your climb.

- **Sun** here? You were born to lead or be seen.
- **Saturn**? You build slow, but leave a legacy.
- **Uranus**? You shake up systems or have an unconventional career.

It also speaks to your **relationship with authority figures** — bosses, institutions, governments, and your parents (often the father).

**Reflect:** What am I building long-term? How do I want to be seen? What's my relationship to success — and failure?

### 11th House: The House of Community and Vision

**Keywords:** Friendships, networks, hopes, social change

This is the **future house**. It rules social groups, activism, communities, your chosen family, and your dreams for society.

It also governs long-term wishes — not to-do lists, but visions for what your life and the world *could* look like.

- **Aquarius** naturally rules this house: collective evolution, idealism, revolution
- **Planets here** can indicate a role in community leadership, social causes, or a wide circle of friendships

This house is also about *belonging*. Are you a lone wolf? Community builder? Quiet visionary?

**Ask:** Who do I align with? What future am I building? Where can I contribute and connect?

### 12th House: The House of the Unseen

**Keywords:** Dreams, soul, subconscious, isolation, spiritual growth

The final house is your **spiritual back room**. It rules your connection to the divine, the hidden, and the subconscious. It's the house of dreams, intuition, endings, karma, healing, and hidden enemies (including your inner saboteur).

This house governs hospitals, prisons, monasteries — places of retreat or surrender. It's associated with both deep healing and potential escapism.

- **Neptune** here can be mystical, creative, or lost
- **Sun** can bring hidden talents or a need for solitude
- **Saturn** may indicate karmic burdens or spiritual discipline

This house is not about ego — it's about soul. And it asks: Where do I dissolve so I can transcend?

**Journal prompts:** What's in my blind spot? How do I restore myself? Where am I avoiding, and where am I being called to surrender?

### House Groupings — Angles, Modes, and Hemispheres

#### Angular, Succedent, and Cadent Houses

Just like the signs have modalities (Cardinal, Fixed, Mutable), the houses have modes of expression too — Angular, Succedent, and Cadent. These groupings shape how the energy of the planets in those houses operates in your life.

**Angular Houses (1st, 4th, 7th, 10th)** — These are the powerhouses of the chart. They align with the Cardinal signs and represent the beginning of action, the birth of movement. Planets in angular houses tend to manifest boldly and visibly.

- **1st House:** How you show up to life — your identity and personal instinct.
- **4th House:** Your roots — the foundation of your inner world.
- **7th House:** Partnerships — where you face another and learn about yourself.
- **10th House:** Your legacy — public image, career, and achievements.

Angular energy is proactive, strong-willed, and attention-grabbing. Think of these houses as the corners of your chart — the architecture that defines your energetic structure.

**Succedent Houses (2nd, 5th, 8th, 11th)** — These houses are the stabilizers. They align with Fixed signs and relate to resources, values, creations, and commitments. Planets here may not shout, but they endure.

- **2nd House:** Personal assets and self-worth.
- **5th House:** Creative projects, children, romance.
- **8th House:** Shared resources, intimacy, transformation.
- **11th House:** Collective goals, friendships, visions for the future.

Succedent energy is about **building and sustaining**. Planets here often indicate where you hold onto things — sometimes constructively (like building wealth or long-term love), and sometimes stubbornly (cue emotional hoarding).

**Cadent Houses (3rd, 6th, 9th, 12th)** — The adapters. These houses align with Mutable signs and support reflection, integration, learning, and preparation for the next cycle.

- **3rd House:** Thought patterns, communication, everyday curiosity.
- **6th House:** Routines, service, health rituals.
- **9th House:** Beliefs, philosophy, long-distance learning.
- **12th House:** Dreams, endings, spiritual retreat.

Planets here are often internalized, less assertive, and may require introspection to fully understand. Cadent houses help you **transition, transform, and synthesize** — like the editors of your life story.

Think of angular houses as **doors**, succedent houses as **walls**, and cadent houses as the **windows** you reflect through. All are essential to the architecture of your chart.

### Hemispheres and Quadrants

Your chart isn't just a flat circle; it has depth — divided into four hemispheres and four quadrants. Each reveals your dominant focus and how you interact with life, others, and your own consciousness.

**Hemispheres:**

- **Eastern Hemisphere (Houses 1–6):** This side of the chart is all about *self-initiation*. It reflects independence, internal motivation, and a tendency to create your own momentum. If most of your planets fall here, you likely carve your own path and don't wait for others to make the first move.
- **Western Hemisphere (Houses 7–12):** This is the "other people" side of the chart. A majority of planets here suggests someone who grows through relationships, cooperation, and responding to life. You may be more aware of how others impact you, or find purpose through partnership and collaboration.
- **Northern Hemisphere (Houses 1–6, below the horizon):** This is the *inner life* zone — rich with private insights, home life, family, and personal growth. People with charts focused here may be introspective, family-oriented, or driven by emotional development rather than external validation.
- **Southern Hemisphere (Houses 7–12, above the horizon):** This is the *public life* arena — focused on achievement, community, recognition, and broader social roles. You may thrive when seen and celebrated, or feel a strong calling to contribute to society in a visible way.

**Quadrants:**

- **Quadrant I (Houses 1–3):** Identity, early environment, and how you self-initiate.
- **Quadrant II (Houses 4–6):** Emotional grounding, service, and personal development.
- **Quadrant III (Houses 7–9):** Relationships, learning through others, expanding worldview.
- **Quadrant IV (Houses 10–12):** Ambition, legacy, and spiritual awareness.

The more planets in a quadrant or hemisphere, the more focus that area will have in your life. It's not about right or wrong — it's about understanding where your soul has chosen to concentrate its growth.

Together, the angularity of the houses, the mode of their operation, and their position within the hemispheres and quadrants provide a 3D view of how your life is architected. It's not just what happens — it's where, how, and why. And when you see the map? You stop walking in circles.

**Putting It All Together**

Your natal chart is a celestial mansion with twelve rooms, each offering a different view of your life. You might host parties in your 11th house, meditate in your 12th, obsess over design in your 4th, and burn out in your 6th.

As you move through life, planets transit these houses, lighting them up like a cosmic spotlight. You'll be called to focus on different areas at different times — and that's the rhythm of growth.

The more you get to know your houses, the more empowered you become to navigate life with intention. Because astrology isn't about fate. It's about *awareness*. And awareness, dear reader, is power.

# Chapter 4: The Planets and Luminaries

*Your Cosmic Cast of Characters*

## Meet Your Inner Solar System

If the zodiac signs are the costumes and the houses are the stage, then the planets are the actors. And oh, what a dramatic ensemble cast they are.

Each planet in your birth chart plays a role in shaping who you are, what drives you, and how you navigate the many plot twists of life. Think of your chart as a personalized space opera. The planets are the ones delivering monologues, sparking love triangles, causing wardrobe malfunctions, and occasionally launching dramatic emotional soliloquies mid-commute.

In this chapter, we're diving into the planets as archetypes — each with its own personality, tempo, domain, and purpose. Some planets act fast and leave a big impression (hi, Mars), while others work subtly over time (hello, Neptune — are you even awake?).

You'll learn what each planet represents, how it behaves when it's happy (dignified) or stressed (in detriment), and why Mercury retrograde isn't actually the end of the world. We'll explore both the personal planets (which shape your personality) and the outer planets (which influence entire generations).

Ready to explore your planetary crew? Let's blast off.

## Personal, Social & Transpersonal Planets

Before we dive into the specifics of each planet, it helps to know what type of energy you're working with. Planets are generally grouped into three categories based on their distance from Earth — and symbolically, how directly they impact your individual psychology.

### Personal Planets: Sun, Moon, Mercury, Venus, Mars

These are your internal tools for navigating life. They're fast-moving, expressive, and shape your conscious personality. If the zodiac is your wardrobe, these planets are how you wear it. They're about your moods, your voice, your passions — all the ways you express "you."

### Social Planets: Jupiter and Saturn

These two orbit a little farther out and move more slowly. Their influence is about your development in relationship to the world. They reflect how you interact with society, handle responsibility, and grow over time. Think of them as the bridge between your personal identity and the broader systems you operate within.

### Transpersonal (or Outer) Planets: Uranus, Neptune, Pluto

These are the big cosmic influencers. They move slowly — so slowly that they influence entire generations. But they still leave their mark on your personal chart, typically representing deep psychological and spiritual themes, as well as transformation on a soul level. You don't always consciously feel them — but when they're triggered, trust me, you'll know.

### The Personal Planets: Your Core Personality Tools

These are the closest to Earth and the most personal. They reveal how you operate day-to-day — how you think, feel, act, relate, and express. They're the planets you're likely most aware of in yourself.

### The Sun: Your Core Identity

**Keywords:** Vitality, self-expression, ego, purpose
**Zodiac ruler:** Leo
**Myth:** Helios/Apollo, the Sun God — radiant, proud, central

Your Sun sign is your inner solar fire — the heartbeat of your personality. It describes your essence, your willpower, your sense of identity. The Sun is your center of gravity. It says, "This is who I am and what I'm becoming."

When your Sun is strong, you radiate confidence and purpose. When it's challenged, you may struggle with identity crises, low self-esteem, or overcompensating bravado.

- **Sun in Fire signs:** Commanding presence, passionate leadership, brave expression.
- **Sun in Earth signs:** Grounded determination, strong sense of duty, self-reliant.
- **Sun in Air signs:** Intellectual curiosity, social radiance, strong opinions.
- **Sun in Water signs:** Sensitive, artistic, soulful depth.

**In the chart:** The Sun's house shows where you shine brightest — where your presence is most needed and most visible.

Live as if you were the Sun — not needing to be seen, but incapable of going unnoticed.

### The Moon: Your Emotional Landscape

**Keywords:** Emotions, instincts, memory, maternal ties
**Zodiac ruler:** Cancer
**Myth:** Selene, Luna, Artemis — guardians of intuition, rhythm, and tides

If the Sun is who you are by daylight, the Moon is who you are in the dark. It governs your feelings, your instincts, and your internal weather system. It's how you process life emotionally and what you need to feel safe.

The Moon is your emotional pulse. It moves fast (every 2.5 days), which is why moods shift quickly. It shows your emotional responses, your early conditioning, and your relationship with mothering energy — both received and given.

12. **Moon in Fire signs:** Big, bold reactions — needs excitement to feel alive.
13. **Moon in Earth signs:** Security-focused — calm, nurturing, but slow to open.
14. **Moon in Air signs:** Detached processing — talks about feelings more than feels them.
15. **Moon in Water signs:** Deep emotional world — intuitive, nostalgic, highly affected.

**In the chart:** The Moon's placement shows how you nurture and need to be nurtured. It's your emotional home.

### Mercury: Your Thinking & Communication Style

**Keywords:** Thought, speech, analysis, perception
**Zodiac rulers:** Gemini, Virgo
**Myth:** Hermes — the winged messenger of the gods

Mercury is the messenger of the cosmos. It governs all things mental: your thought processes, learning style, communication preferences, and even how you text your crush.

This planet also rules short-distance travel and the connections between places and people. Mercury's sign and house show how and where you seek and share information.

- **Fire Mercury:** Bold, fast talker, persuasive.
- **Earth Mercury:** Precise, thorough, skeptical.
- **Air Mercury:** Curious, witty, sharp.
- **Water Mercury:** Intuitive, poetic, and indirect.

### Mercury Retrograde: The Great Cosmic Myth

Let's set the record straight: Mercury retrograde isn't the universe's way of messing with your life — it's more like a cosmic software update. Mercury retrograde doesn't crash your email on purpose or scramble your travel plans out of spite. It's an invitation to slow down, double-check, and reorient.

This phenomenon happens 3–4 times a year for about 3 weeks, and during that time, Mercury appears to move backward in the sky. Symbolically, it's a time when communication, travel, tech, and decision-making require extra care and attention. Glitches, misunderstandings, and déjà vu moments are all part of the experience — but they're not punishments. They're nudges.

Think of it like: The universe tapping the brakes so you don't speed past an important realization.

It's the perfect time to:

- Revisit old conversations and finish what's been left hanging

- Reflect on old ideas with fresh eyes
- Reconnect with people or passions from your past
- Reorganize your space, systems, or thoughts

**What to avoid (if possible):**

- Rushing into major contracts or agreements
- Making large purchases without research
- Jumping to conclusions in miscommunications

Instead of powering through, Mercury retrograde asks you to pause, breathe, and be more intentional. Don't fear the backspin — use it. Some of the best course corrections come when we stop to ask: "Wait... does this actually work?"

Mercury retrograde isn't a cosmic villain — it's the universe handing you a highlighter and saying, "Hey, reread this part."

### Venus: Your Love Language & Aesthetic Eye

**Keywords:** Beauty, harmony, relationships, magnetism
**Zodiac rulers:** Taurus, Libra
**Myth:** Aphrodite — goddess of love, pleasure, sensuality

Venus is how you attract, enjoy, and relate. It's your style of seduction, your taste in beauty, and what you value. It governs your approach to love, connection, pleasure, and yes — your bank account.

- **Fire Venus:** Passionate, theatrical lover. Falls hard and fast.
- **Earth Venus:** Loyal, values stability and long-term partnership.
- **Air Venus:** Loves intellectual bonding. Prefers mental stimulation to clinginess.
- **Water Venus:** Empathic, romantic, emotionally deep.

**In the chart:** Venus shows what (and whom) you're drawn to — and how you show love in return.

**Venus Retrograde:** Every 18 months, Venus retrogrades for about 40 days. These periods often bring major reflection around self-worth, relationships, and personal values. You may reconnect with old flames, question what you truly desire, or give your aesthetic world a full makeover. Venus retrograde isn't just about romance — it's a journey through the heart's underworld.

### Mars: Your Drive & Desire

**Keywords:** Energy, conflict, sexuality, assertion
**Zodiac ruler:** Aries (traditional co-ruler of Scorpio)
**Myth:** Ares — the god of war

Mars is the red-hot force of action. It's how you go after what you want — from careers to crushes to gym PRs. It governs your sex drive, your reaction to conflict, and your motivation style.

- **Fire Mars:** Quick action, explosive energy.
- **Earth Mars:** Persistent effort, practical outcomes.
- **Air Mars:** Argumentative wit, sharp debate.
- **Water Mars:** Indirect assertion, emotional defenses.

**Mars Trouble:** A stressed Mars can be impulsive, angry, or passive-aggressive. A strong Mars is direct, passionate, and fiercely alive.

**Mars Retrograde:** Mars retrograde (about every two years) signals a slowdown in drive and external momentum. It's not about failure — it's about reassessing your goals and the way you pursue them. Tempers may flare or simmer, but clarity comes in the pause. What fuels you? What battles are truly worth your energy?

### The Social Planets: Your Growth & Expansion Tools

These planets act like cosmic professors — they teach you how to grow up, step into society, and create meaning. They influence not only your personal growth but also your role in the broader social systems you're a part of.

### Jupiter: Your Joy & Expansion

**Keywords:** Luck, wisdom, optimism, growth

**Zodiac ruler:** Sagittarius (traditional co-ruler of Pisces)
**Myth:** Zeus — king of Olympus, god of thunder and abundance

Jupiter is your inner YES. It's where you say yes to adventure, knowledge, risk, and new horizons. Wherever Jupiter shows up in your chart, you tend to feel more buoyant, hopeful, and naturally gifted — it's your place of luck and expansion.

- **Fire Jupiter:** Bold, risk-taking adventurer. Expands through courage.
- **Earth Jupiter:** Growth through mastery, patience, and practical application.
- **Air Jupiter:** Philosopher, teacher, and networker. Grows through conversation and connection.
- **Water Jupiter:** Emotional healer, spiritual guide. Expands through compassion and inner vision.

**In the chart:** Jupiter's house shows where you have a natural gift and where growth comes most easily — but also where you might overdo it or get overly idealistic.

**Jupiter Retrograde:** Jupiter retrograde turns the lens inward. It invites reflection on your personal truth, philosophical alignment, and spiritual compass. You may become disillusioned with old beliefs or inspired to redefine what success and joy mean to you.

**Saturn: Your Karma & Discipline**
**Keywords:** Boundaries, structure, maturity, long-term mastery
**Zodiac ruler:** Capricorn (traditional co-ruler of Aquarius)
**Myth:** Cronos — father time, the cosmic accountant

Saturn is where things get real. It doesn't hand out gold stars for showing up late — it demands consistency, effort, and integrity. But once you earn Saturn's approval, the rewards are enduring and meaningful.

Saturn rules time, discipline, hard lessons, and responsibility. It teaches you how to commit, persevere, and build a solid foundation. Wherever Saturn lands in your chart, expect tests, delays, and ultimately — mastery.

- **Fire Saturn:** Must learn to channel passion into steady purpose.
- **Earth Saturn:** Can become overly controlling. Must learn trust and flow.
- **Air Saturn:** Overthinks, underacts. Learns to commit to a path.

- **Water Saturn:** Emotionally guarded. Must set boundaries and process grief.

**Saturn Return = Grow-Up Glow-Up**
Your Saturn Return (around ages 29–30, 58–60, and 87–88) is a rite of passage. It marks a period where you're asked to "grow up" and take responsibility for your life in a deeper, more aligned way. The first return signals the shift from young adulthood into full maturity. It can feel like a breakdown, but it's really a breakthrough.

**Saturn Retrograde:** This period invites you to question your internalized rules, fears, and boundaries. Are you living by your own structure, or someone else's? Retrograde Saturn is less about societal approval and more about personal integrity.

### The Outer Planets: Your Generational Vibe

These slow-moving planets shape the tone of decades and define deep transformation, spiritual evolution, and collective awakening. Their placement in your chart reveals where you experience radical change, inspiration, dissolution, and rebirth. While their influence is often subtle or long-term, they can trigger monumental internal shifts — especially during transits.

### Uranus: Your Inner Rebel

**Keywords:** Liberation, awakening, rebellion, brilliance
**Zodiac ruler:** Aquarius
**Myth:** Uranus — the sky father, agent of revolution

Uranus doesn't knock — it crashes through the window. It's the disruptor of the zodiac, associated with shocks, innovation, and radical change. Uranus represents the part of you that won't be tamed — the genius, the nonconformist, the part that questions why things are the way they are and then breaks them open.

- **In your chart:** Uranus shows where you're uniquely wired to innovate, challenge, and liberate.
- **In transit:** Expect sudden, often uncomfortable shifts that ultimately bring freedom.
- **In signs:** Because it stays in a sign for ~7 years, Uranus represents generational quirks and revolutions (think the rise of the internet or social justice waves).

**Uranus Retrograde:** A time of internal rebellion. You may experience an urge to break free from limiting beliefs or patterns. External change may slow, but inner unrest grows.

Tip: If you're clinging too tightly to a role, belief, or relationship that limits you — Uranus will pull the plug.

**Neptune: Your Dreamworld**
**Keywords:** Spirituality, illusion, mysticism, art, sacrifice
**Zodiac ruler:** Pisces
**Myth:** Neptune — god of the sea, dreams, and vision

Neptune dissolves boundaries. It's where you lose yourself — in love, in art, in dreams. It rules fantasy, compassion, escapism, and divine connection. Neptune governs your spiritual leanings, artistic inspiration, and your soft spot for idealism.

- **In your chart:** Neptune's placement shows where you dream big or become enchanted — for better or worse.
- **In transit:** Neptune fogs and mystifies. You may feel ungrounded or enchanted. Reality may become soft-focus.
- **In signs:** Neptune shapes spiritual and artistic trends for entire generations (e.g., the idealism of the '60s).

**Neptune Retrograde:** This is when the fog lifts. Illusions are stripped away, which can feel disorienting but ultimately enlightening. Truth pierces the dream — and you're left with clarity or heartbreak, depending on what was hiding behind the veil.

Neptune transits can feel like a beautiful dream — until you wake up and ask, "Was that real?"

**Pluto: Your Power & Transformation**
**Keywords:** Death, rebirth, evolution, shadow
**Zodiac ruler:** Scorpio
**Myth:** Pluto/Hades — lord of the underworld, guardian of rebirth

Pluto is the planet of intensity, destruction, and regeneration. It digs beneath the surface and says, “We need to go deeper.” Wherever Pluto sits in your chart, you will undergo evolution, face power dynamics, and experience cycles of loss and rebirth.

- **In your chart:** Pluto shows where you hold hidden power — and where you're called to transform.
- **In transit:** Expect long-term shifts, power struggles, emotional upheaval, and eventual regeneration.
- **In signs:** Pluto governs generational evolution — from collective trauma to shared resilience.

**Pluto Retrograde:** A time to confront your inner shadow. Old patterns of control, obsession, or fear may surface for healing. It’s intense, but it’s where you reclaim your most powerful truth.

Pluto doesn’t ask you to change — it demands it.

### Your Planetary Ensemble Cast

Each planet in your chart is a character. Some are main cast, others guest stars. Together, they form the symphony of you.

- **Sun** gives you purpose.
- **Moon** brings emotion.
- **Mercury** provides thought.
- **Venus** adds love.
- **Mars** offers drive.
- **Jupiter** shows vision.
- **Saturn** sets limits.
- **Uranus** rebels.
- **Neptune** dreams.
- **Pluto** transforms.

Astrology is not a static map. It’s a moving story. And your planetary ensemble is always evolving.

Next up: How do these planetary characters interact with one another? Welcome to **Aspects** — where the plot thickens.

Spoiler: even the hard angles have heart. Especially the ones that yell.

# Part II: The Birth Chart

# Chapter 5: Anatomy of a Natal Chart

*Where the Cosmos Meets You*

## Your Chart Is a Story — Let's Learn to Read It

By now, you've met the planets (your cosmic characters), explored the signs (your character traits), and wandered through the houses (your life's stage). But how do you put it all together into a coherent, insightful chart reading?

This chapter is your decoder ring. We're about to peel back the curtain and explore how to actually read a natal chart. Not like a bored psychic rattling off traits ("You're emotional because you're a Pisces"), but like a cosmic cartographer: someone who sees the patterns, themes, and evolution beneath the surface.

We'll break down the major structural elements of your chart:

- The Ascendant and Midheaven (your public and private entrance)
- The chart rulers and angles (your support beams)
- The layout and glyphs (your astrological alphabet soup)

Once you've got the framework, you'll be able to read any birth chart — yours, your crush's, your boss's (maybe not advisable), or your cat's.

## The Ascendant (Rising Sign): Your Cosmic First Impression

If the Sun is your identity and the Moon is your emotional core, then the Ascendant is your interface. It's the energy you greet the world with — how you show up at a party before anyone really knows you.

16. It's the sign that was rising on the Eastern horizon at the moment of your birth.
17. It changes every two hours, so your birth time *matters*.
18. It determines the starting point of your 1st house and the placement of all other houses.

Your Rising sign is like the filter through which all other parts of your chart express themselves. It governs your body, demeanor, approach to life, and the role you instinctively take on when entering new environments.

A Capricorn Sun with a Sagittarius Ascendant may walk into a room exuding optimism and enthusiasm (Sag), but underneath, they're calculating their next strategic life move (Cap).

It's also the single most visually apparent placement. We often *look like* our Rising signs, or at least dress/express ourselves with their style. Libra Risings radiate symmetry, Venusian grace, and stylish hair. Scorpio Risings have magnetic eyes and an air of mystery. Gemini Risings? Restless hands and a hyper-aware gaze.

Your Rising sign is the cover art of your soul's album. But the tracklist runs much deeper.

### The Midheaven (MC): Your Public Persona and Legacy

Opposite the 4th house cusp (IC), the Midheaven is located at the very top of your chart — the 12 o'clock point — and it represents the highest expression of your public life. The Midheaven (or Medium Coeli) is your cosmic LinkedIn bio, your elevator pitch to the world, and the mountain peak you are trying to climb.

- It tells the world what you aspire to become and how you want to be perceived in the public eye.
- It reveals the tone and style of your career, ambition, public contributions, and social reputation.
- It's the "mask" you wear professionally, in contrast to the Ascendant, which is your personal mask.

While the Ascendant is how you walk into a room, the Midheaven is what you leave behind once you've walked out. It governs not just what you do for work, but *how you define success*. This isn't always a traditional 9-to-5 career — for some, it's becoming a renowned artist, a community leader, or even a deeply respected stay-at-home parent.

**Examples:**

- **Leo MC:** You want to be seen, admired, and remembered. Fame or recognition may not be the goal — but standing out and creating impact is. You're the performer, leader, or creative genius.
- **Virgo MC:** You're here to serve and refine. Your reputation is built on precision, integrity, and being the person who *gets things done right*. You could thrive in teaching, editing, healthcare, or analytics.
- **Pisces MC:** Your public path may appear undefined or multidimensional. You might be drawn to spirituality, healing, the arts, or philanthropy. Others may find your image hard to pin down — but emotionally resonant.

Planets conjunct the Midheaven intensify this area:

- **Sun on MC:** You were born to be visible. Leadership and legacy are your birthrights.
- **Moon on MC:** You're publicly known for your emotional intelligence or nurturing qualities. Your professional life may change with your emotional tides.
- **Pluto on MC:** You might undergo massive career transformations and be drawn to powerful or taboo roles (psychologist, detective, leader in crisis).

Think of your Midheaven as your career's North Star — not a fixed job title, but a guiding principle for how you want to leave your mark on the world.

It's also worth noting that in quadrant-based systems like Placidus, the MC doesn't always fall in the 10th house, but it still holds sway over your professional destiny and how you're perceived at scale. If your MC is in the 9th house, for example, teaching, publishing, or international work may factor into your public life.

### The IC: Your Roots and Private Self

Directly opposite the Midheaven is the IC — the Imum Coeli, or "bottom of the sky." This is the lowest, most hidden part of your chart, representing your private self, your psychological roots, and your literal and emotional home.

- It reflects your early upbringing, ancestral patterns, and how you relate to safety and comfort.
- It reveals what you carry unconsciously — the emotional imprints of your childhood and family lineage.

- It governs your personal sanctuary, your nesting instincts, and how you nurture yourself when no one is watching.

Where the MC shows how you operate in the public world, the IC reveals who you are in your pajamas, curled up on the couch, or returning to your emotional baseline. It's the foundation you rely on — and sometimes the one you must heal.

**Examples:**

- **Capricorn IC:** You may have grown up in a structured, disciplined, or emotionally reserved environment. As an adult, you crave order and stability at home, but may need to work on letting down emotional walls.
- **Cancer IC:** You were likely raised in an emotionally rich environment — for better or worse. You crave deep emotional security in your living space and may build homes that feel nostalgic or family-oriented.
- **Sagittarius IC:** Maybe you moved a lot as a child, or grew up in a home that emphasized freedom, travel, or open-mindedness. You might now crave space, bookshelves, and a home that lets your spirit roam.

Planets at or near the IC influence the foundation of your life:

- **Saturn on the IC:** Indicates early responsibility or emotional restraint. You may have had to grow up fast — but your home later becomes your fortress of discipline and protection.
- **Neptune on the IC:** Your home life may have been chaotic, magical, spiritual, or unclear. You may idealize home, or seek escape there through art, spirituality, or solitude.

Your IC is your emotional attic. You may not look at it often, but everything stored there shapes how you feel safe — or unsafe — in the world.

Healing your IC — through inner child work, ancestral clearing, or building a home that genuinely nurtures you — often unlocks the strength to pursue your Midheaven purpose with more ease and confidence.

In many ways, the MC and IC are two sides of the same coin. You grow into the Midheaven by rooting into the IC. The more securely you know where you come from, the more confidently you'll reach toward where you're going.

### The Four Angles: Foundations of the Chart

The four angles — Ascendant, Descendant, Midheaven, and IC — form the backbone of your chart. They divide the wheel into four quadrants and establish the primary axes of identity, relationship, home, and career.

**1. Ascendant (1st House cusp) — Self:** Your body, instincts, physical and energetic entry point into the world.

**2. Descendant (7th House cusp) — Other:** How you relate to others, what you project, and your one-on-one dynamic.

**3. IC (4th House cusp) — Inner World:** Home, family of origin, your emotional foundation.

**4. Midheaven (10th House cusp) — Outer World:** Career, status, what you're here to build.

If a planet sits on or near one of these angles (within 3–5°), it becomes a major life player. For example:

- Mars conjunct the Ascendant = high energy, assertiveness, possibly confrontation-prone
- Venus conjunct the Descendant = magnetism in relationships, romantic ideals

The angles are your chart's skeleton — everything else builds around them.

### Chart Ruler: The Planet That Steers the Ship

Your **chart ruler** is the planetary ruler of your Ascendant sign. It's the backstage director, the lead engine behind your personal expression. This planet doesn't replace your Sun — it *supports and colors* your entire chart.

**Find your Rising sign and match it to the ruling planet:**

- Aries Rising = Mars
- Taurus/Libra Rising = Venus
- Gemini/Virgo Rising = Mercury

- Cancer Rising = Moon
- Leo Rising = Sun
- Scorpio Rising = Pluto (or Mars, traditionally)
- Sagittarius Rising = Jupiter
- Capricorn Rising = Saturn
- Aquarius Rising = Uranus (or Saturn, traditionally)
- Pisces Rising = Neptune (or Jupiter, traditionally)

Once you know your chart ruler, track *where it is* in your chart (house and sign). This will tell you *how* you approach life.

**Example:**

- Gemini Rising with Mercury in the 10th = Your identity is driven by your career, intellect, and being seen as an expert.
- Leo Rising with Sun in the 4th = You shine brightest at home and value family legacies.

The chart ruler is like the tone of your narration — even if the genre changes, the voice stays consistent.

### Understanding Chart Layouts

Your birth chart is a 360° wheel divided into 12 slices — the houses — and layered with signs and planetary placements. Here's how to decode what you're looking at.

**Anatomy of the Wheel:**

- Outer Rim: The **Zodiac signs**
- Inner Pie Slices: The **Houses** (1 through 12)
- Dots & Symbols: The **Planets**
- Colored Lines: The **Aspects** (we'll cover those next chapter)

Your Rising sign starts at the 9 o'clock position (left horizon). The houses follow counterclockwise.

Different house systems (Placidus, Whole Sign, etc.) may shift house cusps, but the overall layout remains the same. There's no "right" system — try both and see which resonates.

### Decoding Glyphs: Astrology's Secret Symbol Language

Here's a cheat sheet for the core glyphs you'll see in most charts:

#### Planets:

- ☉ Sun ☽ Moon ☿ Mercury
- ♀ Venus ♂ Mars ♃ Jupiter
- ♄ Saturn ♅ Uranus ♆ Neptune ♇ Pluto

#### Points:

- ASC: Ascendant (1st House Cusp)
- MC: Midheaven (10th House Cusp)
- IC: Imum Coeli (4th House Cusp)
- DSC: Descendant (7th House Cusp)

#### Zodiac Signs:

- ♈ Aries ♉ Taurus ♊ Gemini ♋ Cancer
- ♌ Leo ♍ Virgo ♎ Libra ♏ Scorpio
- ♐ Sagittarius ♑ Capricorn ♒ Aquarius ♓ Pisces

These symbols are like emojis from the cosmos — compact but rich with meaning.

### Putting It All Together

Let's say you have:

- **Libra Rising** → Chart ruler is Venus
- **Venus in Capricorn, 4th house** → Your identity is shaped by creating a secure, aesthetically pleasing home. You value deep roots and elegance.
- **MC in Cancer** → You may build a career around caregiving, healing, or nurturing others — maybe even from home.
- **Mars conjunct IC** → Your childhood was marked by conflict or passion. You act from a deep inner place.

Already, we've got a powerful story forming.

Your chart isn't just information. It's integration.

When you understand how all the parts connect — the angles, rulers, placements, and symbols — you start to recognize your own inner operating system.

### You're Not Just a Sun Sign

Reading a natal chart is like learning a new language — at first, you're just identifying letters and syllables. Then, full sentences. Then poetry.

In this chapter, you've learned:

- What the Ascendant and Midheaven are
- Why chart rulers matter
- What angles do
- How to decode layouts and glyphs

In the next chapter, we'll introduce **Aspects** — the planetary conversations that add depth, complexity, and even tension to your chart. Because planets don't just sit in silence. They text, yell, flirt, and collaborate.

And trust me — some of them have *major* group chat energy.

# Chapter 6: Aspects

*The Cosmic Conversations That Shape You*

## When Planets Talk Behind Your Back (Or Hold Hands)

By now, you've met the planets (your cast), the signs (their costumes), and the houses (their stage). But you're not just a bundle of planetary placements lounging around separately — your chart is a web of connections. The planets interact with each other through *aspects*, forming angles that either smooth out your inner world or stir the cosmic pot.

Aspects are how your planets relate to one another — they represent the dialogues, debates, fist-bumps, or silent treatments happening between your various inner voices. One planet might be texting "you up?" while another leaves it on read. Some play nice. Some throw shade. And together? They form the drama that is YOU.

In this chapter, we're going full cosmic couples counseling. You'll learn:

- What the five major aspects are (and why they matter)
- How to work with orbs and aspect strength
- What a Grand Cross, T-square, or Yod means (spoiler: it's epic)
- The difference between easy and challenging aspects
- How to interpret these interplanetary dynamics like a pro

Let's decode the sacred geometry of your soul.

## The Five Major Aspects: Your Inner Planetary Drama

These five core aspects are the foundation of your chart's internal dialogue. They're the most commonly used and most psychologically impactful. Think of them as the interpersonal chemistry between your planetary crew: some are instant besties, some are coworkers with creative tension, and some… well, they ghost each other or throw shade at brunch.

**1. Conjunction (0°)** — The Fused Identity
Planets are side by side, within ~8° of each other. The energies are blended, inseparable, and work as a team (or a codependent couple).

19. This is the most *intense* aspect. Two archetypes are sitting in the same seat, trying to drive the car together.
20. Sometimes it's like a power couple. Sometimes it's a codependent mess. The results depend on *which* planets are involved.

**Examples:**

- Sun conjunct Mercury: Identity and intellect are inseparable. You live in your head and think like you breathe.
- Venus conjunct Pluto: Love and transformation are intertwined. Deep, obsessive feelings, magnetic charm, possibly jealousy issues.

**In a nutshell:** You embody the fusion of these planetary drives — whether it feels like harmony or conflict, you can't *not* express them.

Think: conjoined twins. They share a nervous system. Sometimes they're synchronized. Sometimes they scream at each other in your dreams.

**2. Trine (120°)** — The Flow
Planets in the same element (Fire, Earth, Air, Water), separated by about 120°, forming an equilateral triangle. Trines represent ease, flow, and natural ability. The planets involved understand each other, complement each other, and want to help.

- This is where you're *gifted* — where talents come naturally, often without struggle.
- Trines can indicate lucky breaks, innate harmony, and strengths you don't even realize are extraordinary.

**Examples:**

- Moon trine Venus: Natural charm, emotional warmth, beauty in relationships. Aesthetic gifts.
- Mars trine Jupiter: Boundless energy and enthusiasm. Athleticism, charisma, or success through action.

**Traps of the trine:** Because it's so smooth, it can be ignored. Sometimes the greatest talents in a chart go unused because they don't scream for attention.

Think: a gourmet kitchen you never cook in because delivery is easier. Don't sleep on your trines.

**3. Sextile (60°)** — The Friendly Invitation
Planets two signs apart, separated by 60°, often in compatible elements (e.g., Earth + Water). This aspect brings opportunity and mutual understanding, like two coworkers who don't hang out on weekends, but make magic at the office.

- Sextiles are lighter than trines. They still bring ease, but they need activation — a little elbow grease.
- They show *potential*: doors you can walk through, skills you can develop, relationships you can nurture.

**Examples:**

- Mercury sextile Saturn: Mentally sharp, organized thinker. Great editor, analyst, or planner — *if* you use it.
- Venus sextile Neptune: Romantic idealism, spiritual love, artistic vibes. Lovely for musicians, poets, or just dreamy texts.

**Key advice:** Don't just admire your sextiles. Work them. Think of them as seeds — they need water.

Think: two people flirting in the breakroom. Someone has to make the first move.

**4. Square (90°)** — The Clash
Planets in signs of the same modality (Cardinal, Fixed, Mutable) and 90° apart. This is the tension aspect. It creates friction, inner stress, and the feeling that two parts of you are always fighting for the steering wheel.

- Squares indicate struggle — but also *drive*. They push you to overcome, evolve, and become stronger.

- Without squares, people can get complacent. With too many squares, life can feel like a series of forced therapy sessions.

**Examples:**

- Mars square Saturn: Frustrated will. A lifetime of learning patience, timing, and effective energy use.
- Mercury square Neptune: Foggy thinking, imaginative storytelling — may lie without meaning to. But also potential for poetry and mysticism.

**Productive Squares:** When worked through, squares become engines. They force you to *do something* with the tension.

Think: sparring partners. You'll get bruised. You'll also get better.

**5. Opposition (180°)** — The Mirror
Planets are in opposite signs, forming a straight line across the chart. Oppositions represent polarity — themes of *balance*, projection, and awareness. They tend to show up in relationships, where we attract people who embody what we lack.

- With oppositions, you feel pulled in two directions. It's a teeter-totter, a see-saw — not a war zone.
- You're learning to dance between extremes, without denying either side.

**Examples:**

- Sun opposite Moon: Identity and emotional needs may feel disconnected. Childhood vs. adulthood. Outer mask vs. inner world.
- Venus opposite Uranus: Craves love and freedom at the same time. Often creates a push-pull in intimacy.

**How to master it:** Stop seeing it as a choice between "either/or." Think "both/and." Each planet is valid. The challenge is integration.

Think: two rival roommates in a sitcom. Total opposites, but the show only works when they're both in the room.

**Summary Table: The Five Major Aspects**

| Aspect | Key Traits | Keywords | Examples | Tips |
|---|---|---|---|---|
| **Conjunction (0°)** | Blended, intense, fused identity | Fusion, unity, codependence | Sun conjunct Mercury, Venus conjunct Pluto | Empowering or overwhelming depending on planets |
| **Trine (120°)** | Natural flow, harmony, ease | Talent, grace, synergy | Moon trine Venus, Mars trine Jupiter | Don't take it for granted — activate your strengths |
| **Sextile (60°)** | Friendly, opportunity, latent gifts | Cooperation, effort, growth | Mercury sextile Saturn, Venus sextile Neptune | Requires intention — use it consciously |
| **Square (90°)** | Tension, conflict, motivation to grow | Friction, challenge, sharpening | Mars square Saturn, Mercury square Neptune | Pushes you to evolve through discomfort |
| **Opposition (180°)** | Polarized, mirrored dynamics, awareness | Polarity, projection, balance | Sun opposite Moon, Venus opposite Uranus | Balance both sides — it's not "either/or" |

**Orbs: How Close Is Close Enough?**

An **orb** is how many degrees apart the planets are from an *exact* aspect. The tighter the orb, the louder the aspect's influence.

**General Orb Guidelines:**

- **Conjunctions, Oppositions, Squares**: Strongest within 6° (Sun/Moon up to 10°)
- **Trines and Sextiles**: Usually up to 6°, tighter = stronger
- **Minor Aspects**: 1–3° max

**Tight orbs = signature placements.** Loose orbs still count, but they may fade into the background unless repeated by other chart themes.

Your Moon square Mars at 1°? That's daily life. At 7°? It might only flare up during big events or transits.

### Aspect Patterns: Your Planetary Personality Type

Your chart might contain **aspect patterns** — geometric shapes that involve multiple planets and tell a broader story about how your inner world is wired.

- **Grand Cross (or Grand Square)**
- Four planets, all square each other, forming a giant square/cross
- High internal tension, but **incredible stamina** and long-term power

**Modalities matter:**

- Cardinal = burnout if not paced
- Fixed = stubborn but determined
- Mutable = mentally scattered but adaptable

**Life feels like:** "I can't win — until I learn to master all the moving parts."

### T-Square

- Two planets in opposition, both square a third
- The third planet (apex/focal point) is the "problem-solver"

**Powerful motivator. Tension = action.** Often seen in high-achievers or people with a singular life mission.

**Tip:** Look to the "empty" leg — the sign opposite the apex planet — for balance.

**Yod (Finger of God)**

- Two planets sextile each other and both quincunx a third planet
- Creates a narrow, pressurized focal point of purpose

**A fated, sacred pattern.** The apex planet is your karmic project. Weird, wobbly, and unmistakable.

Think: Soul GPS pointing toward your most meaningful (and often difficult) transformation.

**Kite**

- A Grand Trine with one planet opposite a fourth — creating a "kite" shape
- Natural talent + challenge that makes it soar

**You have a gift — and a reason to *use* it.**

Think: Artist who becomes an activist. Or healer who becomes a leader.

**Grand Trine**

- Three planets in trine — often in the same element
- Sign of grace, ease, and inherited talent

**Element matters:**

- Fire = Creativity, passion
- Earth = Resource mastery
- Air = Mental agility
- Water = Deep empathy, intuition

**But warning:** Grand Trines can lull you into complacency. They must be used intentionally or they gather dust.

**Summary Table: Common Aspect Patterns**

| Pattern | Composition | Key Traits | Growth Opportunities | Challenges |
|---|---|---|---|---|
| **Grand Cross** | Four planets in square, forming a cross | High internal tension, stamina, challenge-drivenit's not "either/or" | Endurance, learning flexibility | Stress, restlessness, inner conflict |
| **T-Square** | Two planets in opposition, both square a third | Pressure to act, pointed focus | Motivation, direction, achievement | Feeling blocked or reactive |
| **Yod** | Two sextile planets both quincunx a third | Karmic mission, odd one out | Soul growth, fate-driven insight | Confusion, awkward growth, delayed activation |
| **Kite** | Grand Trine plus one planet opposite one point | Talent meets challenge, dynamic purpose | Harmonious potential with drive | Needs conscious engagement to thrive |
| **Grand Trine** | Three planets in mutual trine | Natural talent, ease, inner peace | Effortless flow, inherited skills | Complacency, underachievement if not activated |

**Major vs. Minor Aspects: The Main Stage vs. The Nuance**

**Major Aspects** (Conjunction, Trine, Sextile, Square, Opposition): The bold flavors. The lead singers. The plot drivers.

**Minor Aspects:** The subtext. The mood lighting. The background music that changes the scene.

**Quincunx/Inconjunct (150°)**

- Awkward tension between signs that don't relate
- Forces you to reconcile contradictions (e.g., Aries and Virgo)
- Adjustment is required

**Semi-Sextile (30°)**

- Next-door neighbors — not enemies, not friends
- Potential for subtle connection, often unconscious

**Quintile (72°)**

- Creative brilliance. Offbeat genius. Unique expression.
- Especially powerful in artists, designers, musicians

**Septile (51.4°)**

- Spiritual or mystical pull — rare and subtle
- Seen in visionary charts or people drawn to spiritual paths

**Pro Tip:** Don't overanalyze minor aspects until you understand the chart's bigger themes. They're the seasoning — not the meal.

**Summary Table: Major vs. Minor Aspects**

| Aspect Type | Name | Degrees | Keywords | Interpretation Style |
|---|---|---|---|---|
| **Major** | Conjunction | 0° | Fusion, embodiment, unity | Intensifies both planets; they function as one |

| | | | | |
|---|---|---|---|---|
| **Major** | Trine | 120° | Ease, harmony, gifts | Natural talent, flow, requires activation to shine |
| **Major** | Sextile | 60° | Opportunity, cooperation | Potential that needs conscious effort to grow |
| **Major** | Square | 90° | Conflict, challenge, drive | Friction that motivates; learning through tension |
| **Major** | Opposition | 180° | Polarity, relationship, projection | Dynamic tension needing balance and integration |
| **Minor** | Quincunx/Inconjunct | 150° | Discomfort, adjustment | Unresolved tension between incompatible forces |
| **Minor** | Semi-Sextile | 30° | Subtle cooperation or contrast | Low-grade awareness or awkward overlap |
| **Minor** | Quintile | 72° | Creativity, artistry | Unique flair, especially in aesthetics or intuition |
| **Minor** | Septile | ~51.4° | Mysticism, fate | Uncommon; spiritual or destiny-oriented expressions |

### How to Read Aspects in Real Life

1. **Highlight any exact aspects** (within 0–2°). These are loud.
2. **Group aspects by planet.** See which ones are heavily aspected. Those are your busiest archetypes.
3. **Check for patterns.** T-squares and trines tell whole chapters.

4. **Synthesize.** Venus square Uranus might indicate instability in love. But if Venus also trines Saturn? You may crave both freedom *and* structure. The full story lives in the mix.

Don't read aspects in isolation. Read them like a *storyline*. They're connected.

### Aspect Archetypes in Pop Culture

Need a visual? Here's how major aspects show up in your favorite TV dynamics:

- **Conjunction**: Rory & Lorelai (Gilmore Girls) — intertwined, similar voices
- **Trine**: Ted Lasso & Coach Beard — easy rapport, silent communication
- **Sextile**: Monica & Chandler (Friends) — took effort, but had potential
- **Square**: Olivia Pope & Fitz (Scandal) — chemistry meets chaos
- **Opposition**: Mulder & Scully — opposite beliefs, undeniable connection

### Your Aspects Are Evolving

Here's the beauty of aspects: they aren't static. Your natal aspects lay the groundwork, but **transits and progressions** activate and evolve them over time.

- That Moon square Saturn that used to block your vulnerability? It may become your greatest emotional strength.
- That dreamy Neptune trine Venus? It may become the wellspring of your art.

You are not doomed or perfect based on your aspects. You're in dialogue with yourself — for a lifetime.

Astrology is not about fixing yourself. It's about listening deeply to who's speaking inside — and learning how to respond.

Next up, get ready to read the whole thing as a beautiful, chaotic, starlit story.

# Chapter 7: Interpreting a Natal Chart

*Reading the Story in the Stars*

### It's Not Just a Chart — It's a Cosmic Biography

Okay, you've made it through the planets (your cast), the signs (their costumes), the houses (your life's stage), and the aspects (the planetary group chat). But now comes the juicy part — *putting it all together*. How do you *actually interpret* a natal chart in a way that feels insightful, accurate, and empowering?

This chapter is your comprehensive guide to synthesizing everything you've learned. Because astrology isn't just about isolated data points — it's about patterns, meaning, and narrative. It's the symbolic language of the soul. A good astrologer doesn't just regurgitate what each piece means — they intuitively connect the dots to reveal a cohesive story.

We'll walk through:

- How to weave together planets, signs, and houses like a cosmic sentence
- How to identify major chart themes (dominant elements, planetary clusters, empty houses)
- How to read any chart — from a friend's to your own — without freezing up or pulling up 12 tabs
- Step-by-step guidance for approaching birth chart readings with confidence and structure
- Deeper psychological and practical insight for reading beyond personality — into purpose

Let's turn astrology into storytelling.

### A Step-by-Step Guide to Interpreting a Birth Chart

#### Step 1: Know What You're Looking At

Start by familiarizing yourself with the full chart layout:

21. The wheel itself (12 houses)

22. The planets scattered through it
23. The signs on each house cusp
24. The aspects (lines connecting planets)
25. Key points like the Ascendant (rising sign), Midheaven (MC), Descendant (DC), and IC

This overview lets you *visually* absorb the chart's balance and tone before even diving into interpretation.

**Step 2: List All Planet Placements**

Create a basic inventory:

- Sun, Moon, Mercury, Venus, Mars
- Jupiter, Saturn, Uranus, Neptune, Pluto
- Rising sign
- North Node, Chiron, Part of Fortune (optional but helpful)

Note each planet's sign, house, and aspects. Keep a grid handy, or highlight with colors.

**Step 3: Elemental and Modal Balance**

Calculate how many personal planets fall in each:

- **Elements**: Fire, Earth, Air, Water
- **Modalities**: Cardinal, Fixed, Mutable

These patterns give you a first glance into energetic balance:

- Fire-heavy = driven, impatient, enthusiastic
- Air-light = may struggle with detachment or objectivity
- Too much Fixed = stuck in patterns; great for mastery

Most astrologers start by noting if the person is introverted (bottom-heavy chart), extroverted (top-heavy chart), emotionally driven (Water-heavy), or intellectually oriented (Air-heavy).

**Step 4: Start With the Big Three**

These three placements create your personality foundation:

- **Sun**: Who you are learning to become
- **Moon**: What you instinctively feel and need
- **Ascendant**: How you present and initiate experiences

Write a 2–3 sentence interpretation combining each planet's sign and house. Look for:

- Harmony or tension between Sun and Moon
- Whether Rising sign echoes or contrasts the rest
- Whether the chart ruler (planet ruling the Rising sign) is prominent

**Tip**: The house the Sun sits in often shows where your ego is most invested. The house of the Moon shows where you retreat when stressed.

**Step 5: Interpret the Inner Planets**

These reflect your personal style, relationships, and daily habits:

- **Mercury**: Learning, speaking, thinking
- **Venus**: Love, beauty, values
- **Mars**: Passion, action, energy, sexual drive

For each planet:

- Identify its sign and house
- Synthesize its aspects
- Consider its dignity (Is it in rulership, exaltation, fall, or detriment?)

**Example**: Venus in Virgo in the 8th house trine Saturn = cautious with love, loyal in intimacy, builds deep connections slowly but solidly.

**Step 6: Interpret the Outer Planets**

These speak to:

- **Jupiter**: Faith, abundance, beliefs, where you grow
- **Saturn**: Lessons, limitations, fears, structures
- **Uranus**: Rebellion, innovation, sudden change
- **Neptune**: Dreams, illusion, idealism, spiritual longing
- **Pluto**: Power, transformation, trauma, rebirth

Outer planets affect *generations* — but become personal if they:

- Conjunct personal planets
- Reside in angular houses (1st, 4th, 7th, 10th)
- Rule key signs in your chart

### Step 7: Dive Into the Aspects

- Start with conjunctions (strongest blending)
- Look for major aspects to Sun, Moon, Rising, chart ruler
- Use squares/oppositions to identify conflict themes
- Use trines/sextiles to locate natural gifts

Mark aspect patterns:

- Grand Trines = ease, but don't get lazy
- T-Squares = drive, but needs focus
- Yods = odd life paths, mystical growth points

Interpretation tip: Aspects show how your planets *relate to each other.* They reveal your inner conversations — where you're in harmony, and where you argue with yourself.

### Step 8: The House System as a Map of Life

Review each house and look for:

- Packed houses (multiple planets = focus of life)
- Empty houses (read cusp sign + ruler)
- Ruling planets and where they travel

**Key Houses to Prioritize:**

- 1st (Self + life lens)
- 4th (Home/family patterns)
- 7th (Relationships, mirroring)
- 10th (Career, legacy, authority)

Angular houses have the most impact — planets here *shout*. Succedent (2, 5, 8, 11) stabilize. Cadent (3, 6, 9, 12) process and transition.

**Step 9: Spot the Chart Ruler and Midheaven Influence**

- Find the **chart ruler** (planet that rules your Rising sign). Where it lives shows how your life unfolds.
- Examine the **Midheaven (MC)**: Your public image, career identity, and legacy.

A Leo Rising with the Sun in the 6th house of service might serve through leadership and daily support roles.

**Step 10: Pull It All Together — Themes and Storylines**

Now synthesize:

- What's the dominant emotional language (Moon + aspects)?
- What's the core identity challenge or gift (Sun + house)?
- What are the major life themes? (e.g., a chart heavy in the 6th and 10th is work-focused)
- What contradictions exist? (Fire Moon, Earth Sun — impulsive heart, practical ego)
- What placement keeps popping up as a throughline?

Astrology isn't a test. It's a translation. And the best interpretations come from pattern recognition.

**Final Step: Write a Chart Narrative**

Example:

“This is the chart of someone whose mind is always buzzing (Mercury in Gemini in the 3rd house), yet whose heart seeks deep stability (Moon in Taurus in the 4th). There’s a visible charm in how they present (Libra Rising), but underneath is an intense emotional drive for transformation (Pluto conjunct Venus in the 8th). With a heavy 6th house, they’re learning to feel whole through healing and daily acts of service. Saturn square Moon challenges them to regulate emotions and trust others emotionally. Overall, this is a chart about balancing expression with security, independence with vulnerability.”

## Summary Tables for Quick Reference

**Table 1: Natal Chart Interpretation Steps**

| Step | Focus Area | Key Questions |
|---|---|---|
| 1 | Chart Orientation | What am I looking at? |
| 2 | Planetary Inventory | Where are all the planets? |
| 3 | Elements & Modalities | Is there elemental or modality imbalance? |
| 4 | Big Three (Sun, Moon, Rising) | How do core identity, emotions, and approach work? |
| 5 | Inner Planets (Mercury–Mars) | How do I think, love, act, and express myself? |
| 6 | Outer Planets (Jupiter–Pluto) | Where is the generational growth and depth? |
| 7 | Aspects & Patterns | Where is there harmony or friction? |
| 8 | House Themes | Which life areas dominate or feel neutral? |
| 9 | Chart Ruler & MC | How does my life unfold directionally and publicly? |
| 10 | Synthesis & Narrative | What themes and contradictions tell my story? |

**Table 2: Elements and Modalities Summary**

| Category | Traits |
|---|---|
| Fire | Passionate, intuitive, spontaneous |
| Earth | Grounded, practical, methodical |
| Air | Intellectual, social, communicative |
| Water | Emotional, intuitive, nurturing |
| Cardinal | Initiating, driven, proactive |
| Fixed | Persistent, focused, resistant to change |
| Mutable | Adaptable, flexible, scattered |

### Reading the Chart Is Reading the Self

Interpreting a chart isn't about being right — it's about being *resonant*. It's not about memorizing meanings; it's about noticing what themes sing, what contradictions buzz, and what stories emerge.

The chart is a mirror. It's not you, but it shows you who you're here to become.

So grab your notes, trust your intuition, and start reading charts like you're deciphering sacred poetry — because in many ways, you are.

# Chapter 8: Moon, Rising, and the Big Three

*The Core of Who You Are*

### The Three Pillars of Personality

When someone asks you, "What's your sign?" they're usually talking about your **Sun sign** — but that's only one part of the story. Astrology's true magic begins when we explore the **Big Three**: your Sun, Moon, and Rising signs.

Together, these three placements give you the "elevator pitch" of your personality. They represent your identity, your emotional nature, and the mask you wear to greet the world. When interpreted together, they offer a well-rounded view of how you shine, feel, and move through life. Think of them as your cosmic trinity: who you are, how you feel, and how the world sees you.

The Big Three are the starting point of any astrological deep dive. They shape your first impressions, emotional foundations, and personal aspirations. If your entire chart is a symphony, the Big Three are the conductor, rhythm section, and melody — they shape the rest of the music.

In this chapter, we'll explore each of these placements in detail, learn how they interact, how they sometimes contradict, and how to interpret them together for a more complete understanding of the self.

Let's meet your inner trio.

### The Moon Sign — Your Inner World

Your Moon sign governs your:

- Emotional responses
- Subconscious needs
- Instinctual behaviors
- Attachment patterns

While the Sun represents your identity and conscious drive, the Moon shows *what you need to feel safe*. It's where you go when you're tired, hurt, hungry, or falling in love. The Moon describes your emotional language, how you nurture and want to be nurtured.

The Moon is tied to your inner child, your emotional reflexes, and your private self — the version of you that doesn't need to be curated or perform. It can also reflect how you experienced your mother or early caregivers, and what emotional landscape you learned to swim in.

**Water Moon:** Emotional depth, intuition, moodiness.
**Air Moon:** Detached processing, mental clarity, struggles with feeling.
**Fire Moon:** Reactivity, boldness, emotional intensity.
**Earth Moon:** Practical emotions, grounded loyalty, fear of instability.

**Moon in Houses:**

26. **1st house**: Emotionally expressive, wears heart on sleeve
27. **2nd house**: Emotionally anchored in security and comfort
28. **3rd house**: Thinks and talks about emotions frequently
29. **4th house**: Deep ties to home, family, and roots
30. **5th house**: Seeks joy, affection, and play to feel emotionally safe
31. **6th house**: Finds security in routines and being helpful
32. **7th house**: Needs partnership and validation from others
33. **8th house**: Deep emotional processing, privacy, and intensity
34. **9th house**: Finds comfort in spirituality, travel, and philosophy
35. **10th house**: Feels emotionally secure through achievement
36. **11th house**: Connects emotionally through friendships and community
37. **12th house**: Highly sensitive and intuitive, needs solitude to recharge

The Moon is also tied to memory and habit — it rules the past. Many of your reflexive reactions were set by your Moon placement long before you had language for them.

Understanding your Moon is like unlocking your inner child. When your Moon feels safe, you feel whole.

**The Rising Sign — Your Mask and Approach**

Your Rising sign, also known as the **Ascendant**, is the sign rising on the eastern horizon at the exact moment of your birth. It's the front door of your personality.

Rising governs:

- First impressions
- Appearance and demeanor
- How you begin new experiences
- Your lens on life

The Ascendant acts as your social costume — how you show up before people really know you. It often colors your style, body language, voice, and even physical traits.

You might be a dreamy Pisces Sun, but if you have Aries Rising, people will see you as bold, assertive, and dynamic before they ever glimpse your soft interior.

**The Rising Sign also sets your entire house system.** The sign on your Ascendant determines which signs rule which life areas (houses) — that's why an The Rising sign also governs the structure of your **entire birth chart**. It sets the sign on the cusp of the 1st house, which determines the signs on every other house. This is why accurate birth time is essential non-negotiable for chart readings.

**Rising Sign Traits:**

- **Aries Rising**
  Energetic, direct, competitive, confident
  → Comes across as bold, fast-moving, and ready to take action
- **Taurus Rising**
  Grounded, calm, sensual, steady
  → Gives off a composed, dependable, and down-to-earth vibe
- **Gemini Rising**
  Chatty, curious, witty, mentally agile
  → Appears friendly, expressive, and always thinking or asking questions
- **Cancer Rising**
  Caring, intuitive, emotionally attuned, guarded
  → Gives off a nurturing, protective energy, often soft-spoken or warm-eyed

- **Leo Rising**
  Bold, expressive, magnetic, attention-grabbing
  → Comes across as confident, radiant, and theatrically present
- **Virgo Rising**
  Observant, modest, precise, thoughtful
  → Gives off a clean, detail-focused, and service-oriented vibe
- **Libra Rising**
  Charming, diplomatic, graceful, image-conscious
  → Appears polite, stylish, and socially harmonious
- **Scorpio Rising**
  Intense, private, magnetic, perceptive
  → Comes across as mysterious, emotionally deep, and hard to ignore
- **Sagittarius Rising**
  Optimistic, blunt, adventurous, high-spirited
  → Appears open-minded, humorous, and always searching for meaning
- **Capricorn Rising**
  Disciplined, reserved, ambitious, composed
  → Gives off a mature, capable, and sometimes intimidating presence
- **Aquarius Rising**
  Unique, intellectual, aloof, unconventional
  → Comes across as future-minded, quirky, or emotionally detached
- **Pisces Rising**
  Dreamy, gentle, artistic, sensitive
  → Appears soft, empathic, and a bit ethereal or otherworldly

**Chart Ruler:** The planet that rules your Rising sign is your *chart ruler*, and its placement adds important flavor. For example:

- Libra Rising → Venus-ruled chart
- If Venus is in the 9th house, life is filtered through travel, beliefs, and expansion

Each Rising sign is ruled by a planet, and that planet becomes your **chart ruler**:

- Aries Rising → **Mars**
- Taurus/Libra Rising → **Venus**
- Gemini/Virgo Rising → **Mercury**

- Cancer Rising → **Moon**
- Leo Rising → **Sun**
- Scorpio Rising → **Pluto** (and traditionally Mars)
- Sagittarius Rising → **Jupiter**
- Capricorn/Aquarius Rising → **Saturn**
- Pisces Rising → **Neptune** (and traditionally Jupiter)

Rising is how you launch. It's your vibe, your vehicle, your intro music.

**Example**: If you're Virgo Rising and Mercury is in the 7th house in Pisces, you're someone who navigates life through connection and communication, with a poetic or idealistic filter.

Rising is how you launch. It's your vibe, your vehicle, your intro music. And the planet ruling your Rising? That's your personal steering wheel.

**The Sun Sign — Your Identity and Growth Path**

Your Sun sign is the most "you" — your ego, drive, will, and purpose.

It governs your:

- Core personality
- Vitality and life force
- Conscious goals
- Self-expression

The Sun shows who you are growing into. Think of the Sun as the actor behind the mask. It's your lifelong process of becoming. You don't *start* as your Sun sign — you *become* it. That's why people often grow into their Sun more noticeably with age — you grow into it.

The Sun represents what lights you up, what you're here to master, and how you radiate your presence. When the Sun is strong and well-supported, you shine with confidence. If it's under pressure from hard aspects, you might struggle to express your full potential until you've worked through internal conflict.

**Sun in Houses:**

- **1st House:** Personality-centered, needs visibility and personal impact

- **2nd House:** Values-driven, finds purpose through security, possessions, and self-worth
- **3rd House:** Communicative identity, thrives through ideas, learning, and connecting
- **4th House:** Rooted identity, seeks emotional security and a strong home base
- **5th House:** Creative identity, desires attention, expression, romance, and play
- **6th House:** Purpose through service, healing, routines, and meaningful work
- **7th House:** Relationship-oriented, seeks identity through partnership and reflection
- **8th House:** Transformational identity, drawn to depth, intimacy, and emotional rebirth
- **9th House:** Expansive identity, thrives through travel, beliefs, and higher learning
- **10th House:** Public recognition, career-driven, wants legacy and leadership
- **11th House:** Humanitarian identity, thrives in groups, networks, and shared ideals
- **12th House:** Mystical identity, seeks purpose through solitude, intuition, and the unconscious

**Sun in the Elements:**

- **Fire** (Aries, Leo, Sag): Confident, bold, self-driven
- **Earth** (Taurus, Virgo, Capricorn): Steady, responsible, reality-based
- **Air** (Gemini, Libra, Aquarius): Intellectual, communicative, collaborative
- **Water** (Cancer, Scorpio, Pisces): Intuitive, emotionally rich, private

The Sun wants to *shine*. Knowing your Sun sign's gifts and lessons helps you live in alignment with your mission.

**Aspects to the Sun:**

- **Sun trine Jupiter**: Natural confidence and optimism
- **Sun square Saturn**: Struggles with self-esteem, heavy pressure
- **Sun conjunct Neptune**: Idealistic, dreamy, identity can feel blurry
- **Sun opposite Pluto**: Power struggles and deep internal transformation

The Sun is your soul's flashlight. When you follow it, you grow. When you ignore it, you dim.

**The Trio Together — How They Dance**

When interpreting the Big Three, think of them like parts of a team:

- **Sun** = CEO — directs your energy and mission
- **Moon** = Inner Child — signals comfort and emotional truth
- **Rising** = PR Manager — manages impressions and gets you through the door

Sometimes they agree. Sometimes they don't. And that's where things get interesting.

**Examples of Big Three Combinations:**

**Common Big Three Dynamics:**

- **Sun-Moon-Rising in the same element or modality** = harmony, easy sense of identity
- **Conflicting signs (e.g., Water Sun, Fire Rising)** = inner/outer tension, complexity
- **Moon square Ascendant** = inner needs conflict with how others see you
- **Sun opposite Moon** = identity crisis or frequent mood shifts

- **Sun in Gemini, Moon in Cancer, Rising in Libra**
  Your mind is fast and curious (Gemini), your heart is deeply nurturing (Cancer), and you present as charming and graceful (Libra). There's a strong drive for connection, but also inner anxiety about security and belonging.
- **Sun in Capricorn, Moon in Leo, Rising in Aries**
  Outwardly assertive and direct (Aries), internally dramatic and craving praise (Leo), yet driven by responsibility and control (Capricorn). Emotional complexity and leadership potential abound.
- **Sun in Pisces, Moon in Scorpio, Rising in Virgo**
  Emotionally deep and guarded (Scorpio), dreamy and imaginative (Pisces), but shows up as precise and humble (Virgo). Intense inner world, perfectionist exterior.

When your Big Three work together, life flows. When they clash, you're pulled in multiple directions.

**Journal Prompts for Exploring Your Big Three**

- When do I feel most like "myself"? (Sun)
- What makes me feel emotionally safe? (Moon)

- How do others describe me when they first meet me? (Rising)
- Where do I feel misunderstood?
- Which of the Big Three do I identify with most — and why?
- Do my public persona (Rising), emotional needs (Moon), and core self (Sun) support each other or feel disconnected?
- Which Big Three sign is hardest for me to accept — and what can I learn from it?

### Real-World Application of the Big Three

So what do you *do* with this information? Here's how understanding your Big Three can actually make your life better — emotionally, practically, and spiritually:

**In Relationships:**

- Knowing your partner's Moon can help you nurture them the right way
- Their Rising shows how they express themselves early in dating
- Compatibility of your Big Three can reveal communication or emotional mismatches

**Example**: If your Moon is in Cancer and your partner's Moon is in Aquarius, you might feel emotionally distant from them until you learn how they show care through space and ideas, not hugs.

**In Career:**

- The Sun shows your ideal work style (Leo Sun wants to lead or be seen)
- The Moon shows what workplace feels emotionally safe (Taurus Moon needs security)
- The Rising sign influences your professional presentation and first impressions

**In Self-Care:**

- Moon = What soothes you (Pisces Moon needs sleep and art)
- Sun = What energizes you (Sagittarius Sun needs movement and novelty)
- Rising = What centers you when off-balance (Virgo Rising feels better after cleaning)

**In Public Life vs. Private Life:**

- Rising = How you appear in the world, especially on social media or at work

- Moon = How you feel when the lights are off and no one's watching
- Sun = How you want to grow and what you hope people will see

**Summary Table: Traits of the Big Three**

| Placement | Function | Expression | Needs | Challenges |
|---|---|---|---|---|
| Sun | Identity, Purpose | Self-expression, vitality | To shine and feel recognized | Ego imbalance, over-identifying with goals |
| Moon | Emotions, Inner World | Emotional reflexes, comfort style | Safety, nurturing, security | Mood swings, emotional repression |
| Rising | Social Mask, Outer Behavior | How others perceive you | A sense of direction, belonging, flow | Imposter syndrome, misunderstood persona |

**Your Big Three Are Your Foundation**

You are more than your Sun sign — always have been. When you learn to harmonize your Big Three, you start living in alignment with who you truly are.

Your Sun is your core mission. Your Moon is your soul's comfort zone. Your Rising sign is your interface with the world. When one is ignored, life feels off-kilter. When all three are understood, you unlock a deeper level of authenticity.

Whether you feel more like your Moon when alone, your Rising in public, or your Sun in your career — it all matters. You are the sum and synergy of all three.

Understanding your Big Three is like learning the language of your inner world. It's the beginning of every great chart interpretation — and every deep journey of self-awareness.

Next up? We'll take these placements even further as we dive into transits!

# Part III: Beyond the Natal Chart

# Chapter 9: Transits

*Timing is Everything*

## Your Birth Chart Is Not Static

If your natal chart is the blueprint of your soul, then **transits** are the weather patterns that move through your life. They bring seasons of change, growth, tension, and opportunity — all depending on which planets are visiting which parts of your chart.

Transits don't change who you are, but they absolutely affect what's being activated in your life. A transit is simply the movement of a planet in real time, forming aspects (angles) to your natal placements. These angles trigger energies and events — like someone knocking on a door you didn't know existed until now.

Some transits last hours. Others unfold over years. Some feel like a passing breeze, while others feel like a spiritual earthquake. The key is learning to work *with* them rather than against them.

Think of your chart as a clock: the natal chart is the foundation, but transits are the moving hands. Every moment of your life is affected by the planetary dance overhead. Understanding it gives you cosmic timing — an ability to know when to act, when to wait, when to surrender, and when to *grow.*

## What Are Transits?

In astrology, a **transit** occurs when a planet currently in the sky makes a geometric angle (called an "aspect") to a planet or point in your natal chart. These aspects symbolize a conversation between the energies — sometimes harmonious, sometimes tense, always meaningful.

**Transits are the 'now' to your natal chart's 'always.'** They stir up specific themes and prompt you to revisit, revise, or renew parts of your life. Some days feel ordinary. Others feel profound. The difference? Often, it's transits.

## The Five Major Aspects in Transit Interpretation:

- **Conjunction (0°)**: Activation, intensification — two energies merge or collide.
- **Square (90°)**: Friction, challenge, growth through pressure.
- **Opposition (180°)**: Polarization, tension between inner and outer demands.
- **Trine (120°)**: Flow, talent, ease. Like a green light from the universe.
- **Sextile (60°)**: Opportunity, gentle progress, potential that needs your action.

Transits can be:

38. **Exact** — the moment they hit the degree
39. **Applying** — building up in energy
40. **Separating** — fading but still relevant

Knowing which phase you're in can help you make better decisions — and breathe a little easier.

### Inner vs. Outer Planet Transits

Not all transits are created equal. Their intensity and duration depend on how fast the planet moves. Let's break them down:

### Inner Planets (Quick and Frequent)

- **Moon**: Moves every 2–2.5 days — affects moods, energy shifts
- **Mercury**: Every 2–3 weeks — impacts communication, thought, tech
- **Venus**: Every 3–4 weeks — influences love, beauty, money
- **Mars**: Every 6–8 weeks — action, passion, drive

These transits create daily and weekly moods. They're excellent for timing short-term decisions like:

- When to have a difficult conversation (Mercury)
- When you're more likely to feel sensitive (Moon)
- When romance might spark (Venus)
- When conflict might arise (Mars)

They can help you understand:

- Why you suddenly feel irritable or energized
- Why an ex might text you during Venus retrograde
- Why your travel plans derail during Mercury retrograde (because... of course they do)

### Outer Planets (Long-Term, Transformational)

- **Jupiter**: 12-year orbit — expansion, abundance, confidence
- **Saturn**: 29-year orbit — structure, discipline, limitation
- **Uranus**: 84-year orbit — upheaval, innovation, awakening
- **Neptune**: 165-year orbit — dreams, fog, illusion, spirituality
- **Pluto**: 248-year orbit — power, transformation, shadow work

These heavyweights stay in the same sign for years and touch fewer points in your chart — but when they do, *you feel it.*

Think: career overhauls, spiritual awakenings, breakups, breakthroughs, rebirths, ego deaths, re-emergence as a phoenix.

Outer planet transits are rarely subtle. They knock on your door, then bulldoze the driveway.

### Understanding Transits by House and Planet

A transit is most powerful when it:

- Aspects a **natal planet**
- Activates a **natal house**

**Example:**

- Transiting Saturn conjunct your natal Venus in the 7th house = a karmic reckoning in love. You might enter a serious relationship — or leave one that no longer serves you.
- Jupiter transiting your 10th house = professional expansion, recognition, or growth opportunities.

Each planet will bring its flavor to the house it transits:

- **Mercury** in the 3rd = brain on fire, lots of writing, talking, emailing
- **Venus** in the 5th = romantic flings, creative glow-ups
- **Saturn** in the 4th = time to grow up emotionally, restructure your home life

This is why timing is everything in astrology — not just the "what," but the "when" and "where."

### Saturn Returns, Pluto Transits, and Life Cycles

Some transits are so iconic, they have entire books written about them. These are the cosmic coming-of-age moments — the ones we all face, and never forget.

### The Saturn Return (Ages 28–30, 58–60, and 87–89)

Your **Saturn Return** is when Saturn comes back to the same place it occupied when you were born. It happens every ~29 years and signals a massive upgrade in your life — but it doesn't always feel good at the time.

**Common Saturn Return themes:**

- Major breakups or proposals
- Career changes or promotions
- Geographic moves
- Saying goodbye to youthful illusions

It's your soul's way of saying: "You've done the fun, floaty stuff. Now let's build something real."

Saturn asks: Are you living with integrity? If not, it will show.

### Pluto Transits — Death and Rebirth

Pluto moves slowly, but when it hits a natal planet or angle, it *plunges* you into transformation. It's about facing your fears, reclaiming your power, and surrendering to what you can't control.

**When Pluto transits:**

- **Sun**: Identity is reborn
- **Moon**: Emotional depth intensifies; old wounds surface
- **Venus**: Love becomes intense, obsessive, or healing
- **Mars**: Drive is challenged or redirected into power moves

Pluto brings breakdowns so you can rebuild stronger. You'll never be the same afterward — and that's the point.

### Uranus Transits — The Lightning Bolt

Uranus transits shake you out of your comfort zone. It's the planet of surprise, rebellion, awakening.

**Uranus square Uranus** at ~42 years = the classic midlife crisis. **Uranus opposition Sun** = "I can't live like this anymore" moment.

You may:

- Quit your job
- Move cross-country
- Chop off all your hair
- Finally start the business you dreamed of

Uranus wants liberation, not permission.

### Mini Milestones: Other Significant Transit Cycles

### Jupiter Return (~every 12 years)

A time of expansion and optimism. Occurs around age 12, 24, 36, etc. Often coincides with new opportunities, growth spurts, or travels.

### Mars Return (~every 2 years)

Reboots your ambition and energy. A good time to launch things.

### Nodal Returns and Reversals

- **Nodal Return (every ~18.6 years)**: Aligns you with your soul path
- **Nodal Reversal (every ~9 years)**: Pushes you out of your comfort zone and into destiny territory

### Progressed Moon Changes (touched on in Chapter 10)

Your emotional focus shifts about every 2.5 years. Knowing this can explain emotional cycles and evolving priorities.

### How to Read Your Transits Like a Pro

- **Get a transit calendar.** You can use an astrology app or an online chart generator — many platforms offer free daily, weekly, or monthly transit breakdowns. Look for tools that allow you to overlay current planetary movements on your birth chart.
- **Focus on outer planet aspects to your personal planets.** These are the heavy hitters — the long-term, life-changing energies. When planets like Saturn, Uranus, Neptune, or Pluto make contact with your Sun, Moon, Venus, or Mars, something significant is shifting.
- **Track which houses are being activated.** This tells you what area of your life is being affected — whether it's your career, relationships, identity, health, or inner growth. It adds vital context to how a transit may play out.
- **Watch for repeating themes.** When the same kind of challenge, emotion, or opportunity keeps coming up, a transit may be asking for your attention. Astrology loves a good pattern.
- **Keep a cosmic journal.** Jot down what's happening each time a major transit occurs — emotionally, mentally, or externally. These notes become your personal astrology archive and help you decode your growth cycles over time.

### Quick checklist when a transit hits:

- What planet is transiting?
- Which natal planet or house is being hit?
- What aspect is forming?
- What is the element and modality involved?
- What was happening last time this transit occurred?

### Real-Life Examples of Transit Experiences

- **Neptune square Sun**: A client began doubting their career, dissolved their corporate role, and trained as a yoga teacher. Foggy path, spiritual payoff.
- **Saturn conjunct Moon**: Someone experienced emotional withdrawal, began therapy, and set firmer boundaries with family.
- **Uranus through the 7th**: Unexpected breakups, spontaneous new love, deep shifts in relationship expectations.

Each person responds differently. But transits don't invent problems — they reveal and magnify what's ready to evolve.

### Transits and Life Themes

Astrologers often say, "The planets don't *make* things happen — they reflect what's happening inside of us." But transits also teach us about life themes. Each planet teaches its own curriculum when it transits a sensitive point in your chart:

| Planet | Lesson | Shadow Experience | Potential Gift |
|---|---|---|---|
| Mercury | Mindset, communication | Overthinking, tech issues | Clarity, insight, expression |
| Venus | Love, beauty, values | Vanity, indecision, attachment | Harmony, attraction, pleasure |
| Mars | Action, assertion, courage | Aggression, impatience | Drive, determination, passion |

| | | | |
|---|---|---|---|
| Jupiter | Growth, belief, luck | Excess, arrogance | Wisdom, joy, opportunity |
| Saturn | Responsibility, structure | Fear, limitation | Mastery, discipline, resilience |
| Uranus | Awakening, rebellion | Chaos, detachment | Innovation, liberation, originality |
| Neptune | Imagination, spirituality | Delusion, avoidance | Compassion, vision, creativity |
| Pluto | Transformation, empowerment | Obsession, destruction | Rebirth, healing, truth |

Each transit is like a workshop. Some are 3-day retreats (Venus transiting your 5th house). Others are multi-year soul bootcamps (Pluto opposing your Moon). But all ask you to *pay attention.*

**Making the Most of Transit Energy**

When major transits hit, it helps to work *with* the energy rather than resist it. Here are a few ways to integrate different planetary energies in your day-to-day life:

**Rituals by Transit Type:**

- **Saturn transits**: Start a new discipline. Set long-term goals. Organize your finances.
- **Jupiter transits**: Expand your perspective. Travel. Enroll in a course or explore new belief systems.
- **Uranus transits**: Say yes to change. Try something radical. Let go of outdated routines.
- **Neptune transits**: Rest. Create art. Meditate. Journal dreams. Honor your sensitivity.
- **Pluto transits**: Purge what's toxic. See a therapist. Deepen your shadow work or spiritual practices.

**Affirmations for Challenging Transits:**

- "This change is here to awaken something powerful in me."
- "I welcome structure because it creates freedom."
- "Transformation is not loss — it's evolution."
- "I trust divine timing and my ability to adapt."

**Astro-Tracking Practice:**

Create a "Transit Log" for a few months. Note the dates of key aspects, journal what happened, and reflect after the fact. Over time, you'll build confidence in reading your personal timing.

The more you pay attention to your transits, the more gracefully you'll surf the waves of change.

**Time as a Teacher**

Transits are the cosmic clock — they show you when to pause, push, pivot, or plant seeds. They help you align with the natural rhythms of growth and transformation.

Where the natal chart reveals your blueprint, transits show your *timing*. They illuminate your challenges and breakthroughs with divine precision. Even the hard ones are purposeful.

Learn to move with them — not fear them. The more conscious you become of your transits, the more you can work with life, not against it.

Track the skies. Know your seasons. And trust: the universe has its own exquisite rhythm. You were made for it.

# Chapter 10: Progressions & Solar Arcs

*Your Inner Evolution*

### Beyond Transits — Enter the Evolutionary Clock

If transits show the weather of your life, then **progressions** and **solar arcs** reveal the changing seasons of your inner landscape. These tools in predictive astrology are about *becoming*. They map the slow unfolding of your potential, emotional maturity, and soul growth.

While transits tell you what's happening *around* you, progressions and arcs tell you what's happening *within*. They explain why you suddenly crave solitude, become obsessed with writing poetry, or finally understand your childhood wounds — even if nothing external has changed.

Progressions and arcs show the slow-motion evolution of your psyche. And just like a tree shifting from seed to blossom to harvest, your chart evolves over time too. Learning to track these changes brings tremendous self-awareness, patience, and power. Because not everything that matters in life is loud — some things whisper.

So let's decode the subtle but profound language of inner growth.

### What Are Secondary Progressions?

**Secondary progressions** are one of the most widely used techniques in predictive astrology. Here's how they work:

One day of planetary motion = one year of your life.

So your 25th birthday is symbolically linked to where the planets were **25 days after your birth.** Your progressed chart evolves this way, unlocking new emotional flavors, priorities, and attitudes.

Progressions don't predict dramatic events; they chart your internal climate. They show the pace and direction of your soul's growth. You might not notice a progressed Mercury changing signs until you start thinking in entirely new ways. But once you *do* notice? It explains a lot.

**Key Features of Progressions:**

- Focus is on **inner planets** (Sun, Moon, Mercury, Venus, Mars)
- They work best when used alongside transits
- Their influence is subtle but cumulative
- They are ideal for long-range planning and emotional/spiritual insight

Progressions = your soul's slow exhale.

**The Progressed Moon: Your Emotional Cycle**

The most immediately felt progression is the **Moon**. It moves roughly **1 degree per month**, taking **2.5 years to move through a sign**, and about **27-30 years to orbit the full zodiac**.

Because the Moon rules your emotional life, intuition, and needs, this progression tells you what you're craving now, what themes are surfacing, and how your moods are shaped.

**Progressed Moon by Element:**

41. **Fire**: Bold emotions, hunger for self-expression, need for adventure
42. **Earth**: Emotional stability, material focus, body awareness
43. **Air**: Intellectualized emotions, social craving, inner detachment
44. **Water**: Sentimental moods, nostalgia, deep healing

**Progressed Moon by House:**

Each house highlights where your emotional focus is:

- **1st House**: You're reinventing yourself emotionally. A time of personal visibility.
- **2nd House**: You seek safety through money, values, and self-worth.
- **3rd House**: You process feelings by talking, writing, or connecting.
- **4th House**: A major inward turn — healing the past, redefining home.
- **5th House**: Creativity or children become key to your joy.
- **6th House**: You need routine and order to feel okay. Emotional health matters.

- **7th House**: Partnerships take center stage — love or collaboration intensifies.
- **8th House**: Emotional transformation, intimacy, sometimes grief or rebirth.
- **9th House**: You find emotional purpose through learning, travel, or spirituality.
- **10th House**: You pour emotional energy into your career or reputation.
- **11th House**: Friendships and social belonging become central.
- **12th House**: Solitude, retreat, endings, and deep spiritual reflection.

**Progressed Moon Phases:**

Like the natal Moon phases, your progressed Moon phases show what chapter of growth you're in:

| Phase | Keywords | Description |
|---|---|---|
| New Moon | New beginnings | You're planting seeds. Time to initiate. |
| First Quarter | Action | Challenges emerge — you must act. |
| Full Moon | Illumination | A time of fruition or emotional clarity. |
| Last Quarter | Release | Let go of what's no longer useful. |
| Balsamic | Surrender | Rest, integrate, prepare for the new cycle. |

**Progressed Sun: You're Becoming Someone New**

The Sun moves roughly **1 degree per year**, and about every **30 years** it will shift into a new zodiac sign. This marks a major **evolution in identity**.

The sign and house your progressed Sun moves into reveals what your soul is learning to embody — what your "hero's journey" looks like for that phase of life.

**When Your Progressed Sun Changes Signs:**

- You might stop resonating with old goals
- New creative urges appear
- You embody traits of the new sign more naturally

**Example:** Natal Sun in Libra, Progressed Sun in Scorpio:

- You go from peacemaker to truth-seeker
- Charm and diplomacy give way to emotional intensity and depth
- You may attract deeper relationships or confront power issues

Progressed Sun by Element:

- **Fire**: More bold, confident, expressive
- **Earth**: Grounded, practical, long-term vision
- **Air**: Ideas, community, social growth
- **Water**: Intuitive, healing, soul-deep realignment

When your inner light changes hue, the whole world starts to look different.

### Progressed Mercury, Venus, and Mars: Psychological Development

These three are less talked about but still vital. Their progressions reflect:

- **Mercury**: Mindset and communication style
- **Venus**: Love language, what you value
- **Mars**: Drive, conflict style, physicality

**Watch for Sign or Direction Changes:**

- A **Mercury turning retrograde** might pull you inward — more introspective, analytical.
- **Venus stationing direct** could awaken new relationship desires.
- **Mars changing signs** may shift how you go after what you want.

Each change reflects **a new approach to life** — how you express ideas (Mercury), love (Venus), or take action (Mars).

### Progressed Angles: The Soul Shifts Direction

Your Ascendant and Midheaven can also progress and change signs. Though slow-moving, when they shift:

- **Ascendant** = How others perceive you changes
- **Midheaven (MC)** = Your calling or career may evolve

Example: Progressed Ascendant into Sagittarius = you might become more spontaneous, philosophical, or start teaching. If MC moves into Pisces? You may seek creative or healing professions.

### Solar Arc Directions: One Degree, Big Impact

Unlike progressions, **solar arcs** move all planets forward approximately **1 degree per year** — equally and symbolically.

What makes them powerful?

- They time **specific events** or breakthroughs
- When a solar arc planet **conjuncts**, **squares**, or **opposes** a natal planet — pay attention

**Examples:**

- Solar Arc Pluto conjunct Sun = power shift, psychological rebirth, leadership evolution
- Solar Arc Venus conjunct MC = career related to beauty, art, or relationships may bloom

Solar arcs are often used to predict years of **major change**, particularly when exact to the degree.

### Personal Evolution Markers: When You'll Feel It

These moments are less about fate and more about **readiness** — your chart shifts because your soul is prepared.

Top Markers to Watch:

- Progressed Moon changes signs or houses
- Progressed Sun changes signs
- Progressed planet changes direction (retrograde or direct)
- Progressed Moon meets your natal Sun (Progressed New Moon)
- Solar Arc hits your angles or personal planets

Each one brings transformation:

- Old goals melt
- New dreams rise
- Relationships recalibrate
- Creative energy shifts

### Real-Life Examples

- **Client A**: Progressed Venus moved from Aries to Taurus — she left a situationship and began deeply healing her self-worth. A new relationship began six months later.
- **Client B**: Solar Arc Saturn conjunct IC — their mother passed, prompting a reckoning with roots, lineage, and emotional maturity.
- **Client C**: Progressed Sun into Scorpio — became fascinated with trauma therapy, changed careers, and began writing a memoir.

These charts didn't force the outcome. They reflected it — and validated it.

### Charting Your Progressed Growth: Step-by-Step

- **Pull your progressed chart** (and solar arcs if desired)
- **Track your progressed Moon**: What sign, house, and phase is it in?
- **Note any sign changes for Mercury, Venus, Mars, Sun**
- **Check the angles**: Has your Ascendant or Midheaven shifted?
- **Overlay transits** for added precision
- **Keep a progress journal** — reflect on major inner shifts

### Progressions and the Four Elements of the Soul

One of the most revealing ways to track your inner evolution is by examining which elements are highlighted in your progressed chart. If you began life with a fire-dominant chart and now find yourself in a water-heavy progression, you may feel more emotionally reactive, introspective, or intuitively guided than before.

| Element | Progression Focus | Soul Lesson | Internal Experience |
|---|---|---|---|
| Fire | Creativity, courage, renewal | Taking risks, finding passion | Energetic bursts, inspired change |
| Earth | Structure, discipline, embodiment | Grounding dreams into reality | Sensory wisdom, routine craving |
| Air | Ideas, expression, detachment | Rewiring thoughts, connecting minds | Objectivity, social insight |
| Water | Emotion, surrender, intuition | Healing, merging, forgiving | Deep reflection, psychic sensitivity |

Tracking your elemental evolution through progressions can help you understand big shifts in your mood, goals, and even social needs.

### The Astrology of Becoming

You are not who you were five years ago. And you won't be the same five years from now. The natal chart shows your essence — but progressions and solar arcs show who you're becoming.

They reveal what parts of you are emerging, ripening, or being released. They teach patience, self-compassion, and the art of **inner listening**.

It's not about predicting change. It's about growing through it with grace.

Let your chart evolve. Let *you* evolve.

And in the next chapter, we evolve together — through the astrology of relationships.

# Chapter 11: Synastry & Composite Charts

*Love, Connection, and Cosmic Chemistry*

## When Stars Collide (In a Good Way)

Astrology isn't just about *you*. It's also about how *you relate to others* — your lovers, friends, family members, co-workers, and soulmates. This is where relationship astrology comes in, helping you understand the energetic dance between two people.

Welcome to **synastry** and **composite charts** — the two most popular tools in the art of astrological compatibility. While your birth chart reveals your personal wiring, synastry shows how your chart *interacts* with someone else's. The composite chart, on the other hand, reveals the *relationship itself* as a living, breathing third entity.

Whether you're in a situationship, a soul bond, or a sibling rivalry, this chapter will help you decode the energy between you and another person — where you click, where you clash, and how to grow through it.

## What Is Synastry?

**Synastry** is the comparison of two natal charts to assess compatibility, chemistry, and relational dynamics. It's not about judging people as "good" or "bad" matches — it's about understanding how their energy *feels* to you, and what it awakens in your chart.

In synastry, astrologers overlay one chart onto another to examine:

- **Planet-to-planet aspects**: The angles your planets form with theirs (conjunctions, squares, oppositions, trines, sextiles)
- **House overlays**: Where your partner's planets fall in your houses, activating specific life themes
- **Elemental balance**: The interaction of Fire, Earth, Air, and Water in your combined energies
- **Modality harmony**: Whether both people prefer initiating (Cardinal), sustaining (Fixed), or adapting (Mutable) styles

These layers tell us where there's ease, where there's tension, and where the sparks fly (or misfire).

**Top Aspects to Look For:**

45. **Sun-Moon aspects**: Shared identity and emotional bonding; often found in long-term partnerships
46. **Venus-Mars aspects**: Sexual chemistry, physical attraction, the romantic spark
47. **Moon-Moon or Moon-Venus**: Deep emotional compatibility, comfort, and care
48. **Mercury aspects**: The quality of conversation and ability to resolve conflict verbally
49. **Saturn aspects**: Indicators of long-term bonds, responsibilities, or karma — can feel grounding or heavy
50. **Uranus, Neptune, Pluto aspects**: Intensity, soul connections, chaos, or spiritual lessons; these can be felt as fate, fantasy, or frustration

Every relationship has friction. Synastry shows whether it's fire-building or fire-destroying.

**House Overlays: Where They Land in Your Life**

When you overlay someone's planets onto your natal chart, you see where they activate your life areas (houses). These placements show *how* they affect you — and which parts of your life they stir up.

**Key House Overlay Examples:**

- **1st House**: Their presence affects your identity, confidence, and self-image. They see you clearly — or project an ideal.
- **4th House**: They feel like home or family. Deep emotional resonance and comfort — or enmeshment.
- **5th House**: Romantic, creative, or childlike energy. They awaken your playfulness, self-expression, and desire.

- **7th House**: Long-term partnership potential. They reflect who you're seeking in a spouse or collaborator.
- **8th House**: Sexual intensity, emotional bonding, psychological triggers. Deep trust issues or soul merging can occur.
- **10th House**: They influence your public image or career. You may admire or feel challenged by their authority.

House overlays reveal what *role* someone plays in your life — muse, mentor, mirror, or mystery.

### Compatibility Isn't Perfection — It's Chemistry

True compatibility is complex. It's not about avoiding conflict — it's about knowing *how* and *why* conflict arises, and having the tools to move through it. Astrology helps you:

- See how the other person *receives* your energy
- Understand emotional mismatches (e.g., a Leo Moon may need attention, while a Capricorn Moon needs control)
- Decode recurring arguments (e.g., Mars square Mars = clashing motivations)
- Know where your values, needs, and dreams align (or diverge)

Even "hard" aspects in synastry, like Moon square Saturn or Venus opposite Pluto, aren't deal-breakers. They simply mean the relationship requires conscious work and evolution.

Compatibility doesn't mean comfort — it means **awareness and willingness**.

### The Composite Chart: Your Relationship as a Third Entity

While synastry compares two charts directly, a **composite chart** combines them into a single, symbolic chart. It's calculated by finding the *midpoints* between your planets — literally the average between both charts' placements.

The result is the chart of the relationship itself. It answers:

- What is this relationship here to teach us?
- How do we express love, anger, support *together*?

- What is our shared destiny?

**Key Composite Chart Points:**

- **Composite Sun**: The purpose and identity of the relationship
- **Composite Moon**: Shared emotional energy and patterns
- **Composite Venus**: The way you express affection and beauty as a couple
- **Composite Mars**: How you take action or experience conflict as a unit
- **Composite Saturn**: The structure, commitment, and limitations of the relationship
- **Composite North Node**: The evolutionary path and purpose of the bond

Composite chart placements *aren't* a sum of your individual personalities — they describe the alchemy that emerges *only* when you come together.

### Synastry vs. Composite: When to Use Each

| **Use Synastry to...** | **Use Composite to...** |
|---|---|
| Understand individual attraction | Understand the relationship's soul purpose |
| See where you challenge or comfort each other | See how the relationship functions over time |
| Compare communication styles | Learn how your combined energy impacts the world |
| Spot emotional triggers and growth areas | Determine the overall vibe of the union |

Synastry is like a duet. Composite is the entire relationship's soundtrack.

### Family, Friends & Other Bonds

Relationship astrology applies to *all* bonds — not just romantic ones.

- **Parent-child** synastry can reveal how you nurture, trigger, or protect each other
- **Sibling** synastry often reflects rivalry, roles, or karmic mirroring
- **Friendship** synastry might show easy Mercury or Venus connections, or shared North Node activations
- **Work or business partnerships** benefit from strong Saturn, Mercury, and 10th house overlays

You can also compare composite charts between friends or colleagues to understand the essence of the relationship — is it collaborative, competitive, karmic, or temporary?

### Synastry Red Flags vs. Growth Points

Let's be clear: no aspect is automatically a deal-breaker. But some require *awareness and emotional maturity*.

| **Red Flag Aspect** | **Meaning** | **What to Watch** |
|---|---|---|
| Mars square Mars | Conflict styles clash | Frequent arguments, power struggles |
| Saturn conjunct Moon | Emotional suppression | Coldness, guilt, long-term tests |
| Neptune square Venus | Romantic confusion | Idealizing or not seeing clearly |
| Pluto opposite Sun | Power imbalance | Control issues, obsession, compulsion |

### Growth Opportunities:

- Saturn aspects: Teach structure, commitment, and long-term effort
- Pluto aspects: Intimacy, shadow work, transformation
- Uranus aspects: Change, awakening, shaking off old patterns
- Chiron aspects: Healing each other's wounds with compassion

A red flag doesn't mean stop. It means slow down and get honest.

### How to Read a Relationship Chart (Step-by-Step)

- **Pull both natal charts**: Note the dominant elements, modalities, and planets
- **Overlay the charts** (synastry): Focus on aspects between personal planets
- **Examine house overlays**: See where their planets fall in your life
- **Look for repeating themes**: Do certain houses or elements get lit up?
- **Pull the composite chart**: Understand the "third energy"
- **Assess overall tone**: Is the chart heavy with squares? Or full of trines?

You'll begin to sense the difference between:

- Soul contracts and comfort connections
- Relationships meant for lessons vs. lifetimes
- Patterns you need to break — and ones you're here to build

### Timing in Relationship Astrology

While synastry and composite charts show compatibility and dynamics, **timing** adds another layer of depth. Transits and progressions to the composite chart or to key planets in each individual's chart can trigger major relationship shifts.

**Common Timing Triggers:**

- **Saturn transiting Venus (in composite or synastry)**: Tests love, commitment, and values. May bring separation or maturity.
- **Uranus transiting the composite Sun or Ascendant**: Shocks, breakups, or exciting new directions. Sudden independence.
- **Neptune to the composite Moon or Venus**: Dreamy romance or confusion. May need to clarify illusions.
- **Pluto conjunct personal planets**: Deep transformation or power struggles. Soul-level change.

Astrology can help you prepare for these cycles by showing what kinds of energy are being activated and how best to work with them. Just like with personal transits, these influences don't dictate outcomes — they reflect opportunities for conscious evolution within your connection.

### Cosmic Chemistry

Love isn't always logical. But astrology gives us language for the inexplicable — for why someone feels like home, why another pushes every button, or why some bonds change us forever.

Synastry doesn't predict success. It reveals patterns, potentials, and pressure points. The rest is up to you.

So whether you're in a soulmate union, a karmic spiral, or a lifelong friendship — astrology helps you navigate it with eyes wide open and heart aligned.

Because when stars collide with intention, connection becomes destiny.

# Chapter 12: Nodes and Karma

*Soul Contracts and Life Lessons*

### The Moon's Shadow, Your Soul's Map

If your Sun sign is the *who*, your Moon sign is the *how*, and your Rising sign is the *what first*, then your **Lunar Nodes** are the *why*. Why are you here? What are you meant to release? What are you meant to grow into? That's the terrain of the **North Node** and **South Node** — a mystical axis of soul evolution.

The Nodes don't represent planets. They are **mathematical points** — where the Moon's orbit crosses the Sun's path (the ecliptic). But their symbolism is powerful. The **South Node** (also called Ketu in Vedic astrology) represents your past: familiar energies, talents you've mastered, comfort zones, and karma. The **North Node** (Rahu in Vedic terms) points to your soul's purpose: the unfamiliar, the stretching zone, the direction of spiritual growth.

Your nodal axis isn't just about personality — it's about soul evolution. It's not about who you are. It's about who you're becoming.

In this chapter, we'll explore how to interpret the Nodes in your chart, what each sign and house placement means, how transits to the Nodes activate life shifts, and how nodal dynamics affect relationships.

### The Basics: North Node vs. South Node

| Node | Symbolizes | Keywords | Emotional Tone |
|---|---|---|---|
| South Node | Past life patterns, karmic inheritance, overused gifts | Comfort, habit, detachment, release | Familiar but draining |
| North Node | Soul path, life mission, growth edge | Destiny, purpose, longing, challenge | Uncomfortable but energizing |

**Think of it like this:**

- South Node = Your favorite old sweater. Cozy but worn out.
- North Node = A fabulous coat that doesn't quite fit — yet.

Your job isn't to *abandon* the South Node — it's to integrate its strengths while moving toward the North.

### Nodal Signs and Soul Themes

Each nodal axis teaches a particular lesson. Here's a sample of what each pairing asks of you:

| Nodal Axis | Soul Lesson |
|---|---|
| Aries–Libra | From people-pleasing to self-leadership |
| Taurus–Scorpio | From control/fear to trust and embodiment |
| Gemini–Sagittarius | From certainty to curiosity and nuance |
| Cancer–Capricorn | From emotional detachment to heart-centered maturity |
| Leo–Aquarius | From fitting in to shining your unique light |
| Virgo–Pisces | From chaos or martyrdom to spiritual order and service |

Remember, the **South Node shows what comes easily** — but may hold you back. The **North Node feels foreign** — but holds your evolutionary key.

### Nodal Houses: The Life Arenas

The **houses** show *where* the nodal lessons unfold:

51. **1st/7th**: From merging with others to self-definition (or vice versa)

52. **2nd/8th**: From shared resources to self-sufficiency (or vice versa)
53. **3rd/9th**: From abstract beliefs to lived experience (or vice versa)
54. **4th/10th**: From public ambition to emotional roots (or vice versa)
55. **5th/11th**: From collective roles to creative self-expression (or vice versa)
56. **6th/12th**: From personal sacrifice to practical service (or vice versa)

Your soul's classroom is the house of your North Node. Show up there. Study hard.

### Nodal Returns and Reversals

Your **Nodal Return** happens around ages **18–19**, **37–38**, **56–57**, and so on. It's a time when your soul reaffirms its growth path — often through choices or awakenings that feel strangely fated.

A **Nodal Reversal** (when transiting Nodes oppose your natal ones) happens around ages **9, 27, 46, 65**, etc. These bring up old patterns and test your ability to stay on course.

Nodal returns say, "Step up." Nodal reversals ask, "Have you really changed?"

### Karmic Relationships: When Your Nodes Meet Theirs

In synastry, nodal connections often feel magnetic — like you've known the person forever. They trigger past-life themes and future-life lessons:

- **Your South Node conjunct their planet**: They feel familiar, but may keep you in your comfort zone.
- **Your North Node conjunct their planet**: They pull you toward growth — even if it's uncomfortable.

In composite charts, Nodes tell the story of the relationship's purpose:

- **North Node in the 4th house**: This relationship is about emotional grounding.
- **South Node in the 10th house**: Let go of status and public performance — build a home instead.

Not all karmic relationships are forever. Some are bridges. Some are soul contracts with expiration dates.

### Transits and Nodal Activation

When **planets transit your Nodes**, major life shifts can occur:

- **Saturn conjunct the North Node**: Time to take responsibility for your purpose. Serious growth moment.
- **Jupiter conjunct the North Node**: Destiny calling — expansion aligned with your soul path.
- **Pluto on your South Node**: Deep release of karmic patterns. Soul detox.

Likewise, when **transiting Nodes** hit your personal planets or angles (Sun, Moon, Ascendant, MC), pay attention. Events may seem fated, meetings serendipitous, and choices heavier with meaning.

### Working with the Nodes: A Practice

Here are ways to consciously engage your nodal path:

- **Reflect**: What themes keep repeating? Where do you feel stuck? That's South Node terrain.
- **Challenge**: Where do you feel drawn, even if it scares you? That's North Node guidance.
- **Journal**: "When I honor my North Node, I feel..." / "When I cling to my South Node, I..."
- **Affirm**: "I trust my discomfort. I am becoming."

Walking the nodal path is less about perfection and more about direction.

### Nodal Polarity in Practice

One of the most empowering ways to embody your nodal path is to recognize the **polarity** at play. The South and North Nodes are always opposite signs, so your work is not to reject one and embrace the other — it's to **balance them**.

Here's how that looks in practice:

| Axis | Shadow of South Node | Strength of South Node | Gift of North Node |
|---|---|---|---|
| Aries–Libra | Aggression, selfishness | Courage, independence | Harmony through assertiveness |
| Taurus–Scorpio | Stagnation, materialism | Sensuality, loyalty | Transformation, emotional depth |
| Gemini–Sagittarius | Gossip, indecision | Wit, communication | Wisdom, big-picture thinking |
| Cancer–Capricorn | Clinging to the past | Nurturing, emotional intelligence | Ambition, maturity, stability |
| Leo–Aquarius | Ego, vanity | Confidence, creativity | Vision, collaboration, innovation |
| Virgo–Pisces | Perfectionism, judgment | Dedication, skill | Compassion, surrender, spiritual trust |

Knowing your nodal polarity helps you identify where you lean too hard — and where you're being asked to grow.

**Example Practice: Living the Virgo–Pisces Axis**

- **South Node in Virgo** may feel safer with rules and structure, avoiding emotional messiness.
- But **North Node in Pisces** asks you to soften into trust, art, and spiritual faith — to let go of having all the answers.

Your growth happens where your logic ends and your heart begins.

### Integrating the Nodes into Your Daily Life

Understanding the Nodes is one thing — *living* them is another. Your nodal axis isn't a "one and done" event. It's a lifelong journey of incremental evolution, choice by choice, year by year.

Here are some grounded ways to align with your nodal path daily:

#### 1. Set Nodal Intentions by Sign and House

Each month, set a small, symbolic goal related to your North Node sign and house. For example:

- **North Node in Leo in the 5th house**: Set an intention to express yourself creatively — write a poem, dance in your living room, post that selfie.
- **North Node in Capricorn in the 10th house**: Make a tangible step toward a career goal — submit a resume, declare a boundary, plan your legacy.

#### 2. Use Lunar Cycles to Support Nodal Growth

- **New Moon near your North Node**: Plant seeds that align with your soul's purpose
- **Full Moon near your South Node**: Acknowledge and release old habits and emotional crutches

#### 3. Meditate with Your Nodes

In a quiet space, visualize your South Node energy as a familiar old room you're preparing to leave. Thank it. Then imagine your North Node as a distant glowing door — unknown, but calling. Feel yourself stepping toward it, even if you're afraid. Repeat: "I trust my soul's direction."

#### 4. Track Nodal Transits in Real Time

Create a nodal journal to track:

- When the transiting Nodes aspect your personal planets
- When eclipses fall on your Nodes (these are *major* karmic pivots!)
- Your internal reactions: What's surfacing? What's falling away?

### 5. Talk to Your Past and Future Selves

Write a letter from your South Node to your North Node. Let it voice its fears, memories, and pride. Then write back — as your North Node — offering encouragement, curiosity, and light. Let this be a healing ritual.

The Nodes don't ask you to be someone else. They ask you to remember who you came here to become.

## A North Node Awakening in Real Life

Let's bring the Nodes to life with an example.

**Ella** was born with her North Node in **Aquarius in the 11th house**, and her South Node in **Leo in the 5th**. Growing up, she was the center of attention: theater kid, class president, endlessly praised for her charisma. But in her late 20s, she felt restless. Her dreams of acting didn't inspire her anymore. Fame felt hollow.

She began volunteering at a local nonprofit. What started as part-time turned into full-time — and eventually, she launched a community program that brought arts education to underserved youth.

For the first time, she didn't care about being in the spotlight. She wanted to uplift others. That's classic 5th house Leo to 11th house Aquarius evolution: from personal glory to collective impact.

"I stopped needing applause," she said. "I started needing purpose."

Your North Node will whisper to you until it roars. It will guide you from who you've been to who the world needs you to become.

## The Compass of the Soul

Your natal chart is a map. But the **Nodes are the compass** — they show you which way to walk. Not to escape who you've been, but to become more fully who you were always meant to be.

Don't fear the unknown of your North Node. Trust that your soul knew what it was doing when it pointed in that direction. And let the South Node be a reminder that you've already come so far — and it's okay to let go.

You are not lost. You are becoming.

And with that, we close Part III of your astrological journey.

Ahead? The celestial depths of Part IV — where asteroids, Lilith, and cosmic shadow work await.

# Part IV: Specialized Astrology

# Chapter 13: Asteroids and Chiron

*Healing, Archetypes, and the Deep Details*

### Beyond the Planets — Enter the Cosmic Fine Print

If planets are the main cast of your astrological drama, then **asteroids and Chiron** are the recurring characters that steal the scene. They may be smaller, but they bring flavor, nuance, and depth. They reveal the complexities that don't always show up in planetary interpretations — stories of healing, devotion, intellect, sacrifice, and relationship wounds.

In this chapter, we'll meet five of the most influential asteroids — **Chiron, Ceres, Pallas, Vesta, and Juno** — and explore how they add nuance to your natal chart. These celestial bodies are deeply symbolic, often tied to mythological figures, and offer insight into spiritual purpose, emotional patterns, and karmic themes.

Let's dive into the subtle forces that help complete the cosmic picture.

### Chiron: The Wounded Healer

**Keywords:** Wound, wisdom, integration, sacred pain

Chiron reveals the place in your chart where you carry a wound so deep, it feels ancient — a kind of soul-soreness that resists easy explanation or resolution. It's not just emotional pain; it's the type of ache that shapes how you see yourself and what you believe you must hide or fix in order to be loved. And yet, Chiron is also where you have the most to offer others — because your pain becomes your path to empathy, purpose, and healing.

This is the paradox of Chiron: the very thing that makes you feel broken is also what makes you wise. When acknowledged rather than avoided, this wound becomes a bridge — not only to self-acceptance but to becoming a guide for others walking similar paths.

**Mythology:**
In Greek mythology, Chiron was a centaur — half-man, half-horse — famed as a wise healer and teacher of heroes. Despite his ability to heal others, he couldn't heal his own wound. This archetype reflects how we often help others through the very pain we carry ourselves.

**Chiron in Your Chart Shows:**

- Where you feel fundamentally flawed
- What you hide or overcompensate for
- How you can guide others through similar pain

**Themes by Sign:**

57. **Aries**: Wounds around assertion or selfishness; healing through courage
58. **Taurus**: Insecurity around self-worth or stability; healing through grounding
59. **Gemini**: Fear of being misunderstood; healing through authentic voice
60. **Cancer**: Emotional pain tied to family or safety; healing through self-parenting
61. **Leo**: Wounds around recognition or creative visibility; healing through self-love
62. **Virgo**: Pain around inadequacy or over-functioning; healing through service
63. **Libra**: Struggles with fairness and partnership; healing through reciprocity
64. **Scorpio**: Wounds of betrayal, loss, or emotional depth; healing through transformation
65. **Sagittarius**: Pain linked to belief, meaning, or freedom; healing through exploration
66. **Capricorn**: Fear of failure or not being "enough"; healing through self-respect
67. **Aquarius**: Wounds around exclusion or difference; healing through radical self-acceptance
68. **Pisces**: Pain linked to sacrifice or disillusionment; healing through spiritual compassion

Chiron reminds us that pain is not a flaw in the system — it's part of the design. The places we feel unworthy, unseen, or ashamed are not meant to be erased, but embraced. They are portals to compassion, connection, and purpose. Through Chiron, we learn that healing isn't about becoming perfect — it's about becoming whole. And in that wholeness, we become a light for others, offering the very medicine we once needed ourselves.

**Ceres: The Nurturer**

**Keywords:** Mothering, loss, cycles, nourishment

Ceres symbolizes how we give and receive nourishment — not just in terms of food or care, but also in our emotional rhythms, attachments, and the ability to let go when needed. She speaks to the sacred balance of holding and releasing, of feeding others and remembering to feed ourselves.

This asteroid governs our relationship with the cycles of love — how we cope with absence, how we grieve, and how we return to love again. She's connected to parenting, caregiving, body-based comfort, and the emotional importance of feeling held, safe, and supported.

**Mythology:**
Ceres, the Roman counterpart of Demeter, was the mother goddess who lost her daughter Persephone to the underworld. Her sorrow brought winter; her joy, spring. Through her, we experience the emotional tides of connection, separation, and reunion.

**In Your Chart, Ceres Shows:**

- Your caregiving style and nourishment needs
- How you handle loss, separation, and reunion
- Your emotional relationship to food, safety, and belonging

**Themes by Sign:**

- **Aries**: Protective, action-oriented caregiver; needs autonomy
- **Taurus**: Steady, sensory nurturing; needs security
- **Gemini**: Communicative care; needs verbal connection
- **Cancer**: Deeply maternal and protective; needs emotional safety
- **Leo**: Joyful, celebratory nurturer; needs admiration and attention
- **Virgo**: Detail-oriented and service-based; needs to feel useful
- **Libra**: Graceful and balanced caregiver; needs harmony
- **Scorpio**: Intense, loyal nurturer; needs trust and emotional honesty
- **Sagittarius**: Philosophical, freedom-based caregiver; needs meaning and space
- **Capricorn**: Structured, dependable nurturer; needs respect and stability
- **Aquarius**: Idealistic, collective-focused; needs authenticity and acceptance
- **Pisces**: Compassionate and sacrificial nurturer; needs spiritual and emotional resonance

Ceres reminds us that real love includes loss, and that nourishment is both an offering and a need. She teaches us to honor the seasons of the heart — the times of abundance, the winters of grief, and the sacred act of returning. Her wisdom lives in the quiet moments of care, in the meals prepared with love, in the tears we shed when someone is gone, and in the strength it takes to open our arms again. Through Ceres, we learn that to nurture is to risk loss — and to love anyway.

### Pallas: The Strategic Warrior

**Keywords:** Wisdom, intelligence, pattern recognition, justice

Pallas is your inner strategist — the part of you that notices patterns, finds elegant solutions, and fights not with force, but with intelligence and insight. She governs how you analyze complexity, resolve conflicts, and use your mind to defend what matters to you.

While Mars fights on instinct, Pallas fights with foresight. She represents your mental clarity, symbolic intelligence, and how you link logic with creativity. Whether in relationships, art, activism, or career, Pallas shows how you cut through chaos to bring order and wisdom.

**Mythology:**
Born fully armored from Zeus's head, Pallas Athena was the goddess of war and wisdom — yet she fought with intellect, not brute force. Patron of artisans, lawyers, and tacticians, she embodies mental clarity and creative insight.

**Pallas in Your Chart Shows:**

- How you approach complex problems and conflicts
- Where you apply wisdom in relationships, work, or politics
- Your unique form of feminine intelligence and strategic expression

**Themes by Sign:**

- **Aries**: Bold, instinctive strategist; acts fast
- **Taurus**: Grounded thinker; practical and artistic
- **Gemini**: Verbal problem-solver; thrives on ideas
- **Cancer**: Emotionally perceptive strategist; reads people well

- **Leo**: Charismatic visionary; leads with flair
- **Virgo**: Analytical and precise; excels at systems
- **Libra**: Diplomatic tactician; balances justice and harmony
- **Scorpio**: Deep psychological strategist; sees hidden motives
- **Sagittarius**: Ethical problem-solver; guided by principles
- **Capricorn**: Planner with foresight; organizes for success
- **Aquarius**: Innovative and big-picture thinker; serves collective
- **Pisces**: Intuitive, artistic strategist; feels patterns into place

Pallas teaches that real power comes from perception, not domination. She is the cosmic tactician — the part of you that sees the whole board, not just the next move. Where others react, she strategizes. Where others get lost in the noise, she sees the board, identifies the pattern, and plans accordingly. Pallas adds a layer of intellectual elegance to your cosmic blueprint, reminding you that wisdom is the highest form of strength.

### Vesta: The Sacred Flame

**Keywords:** Focus, dedication, inner fire, sacred sexuality

Vesta represents what you commit to with full devotion — the cause, practice, or space that feels sacred. She speaks to your ability to focus your energy, set boundaries, and remain true to a deeper calling, even in solitude.

This asteroid also touches on your relationship with sexuality — not as mere pleasure, but as a form of spiritual power. Vesta governs the temple of the self: the part of you that stays lit even when everything else fades.

**Mythology:**
Vesta, known as Hestia in Greek myth, was goddess of the hearth — keeper of the eternal flame. Her priestesses remained celibate to preserve their focus, embodying full devotion to spiritual service. She represents purity of purpose.

**In Your Chart, Vesta Reveals:**

- Your sacred focus — where you commit fully and protect fiercely
- How you manage solitude, sexuality, and energy boundaries
- The cause, calling, or space that deserves your undivided attention

**Themes by Sign:**

- **Aries**: Devotion to action, boldness, and leadership
- **Taurus**: Loyalty to pleasure, stability, and sensuality
- **Gemini**: Commitment to curiosity, language, and thought
- **Cancer**: Dedication to emotional sanctuary and home
- **Leo**: Fierce loyalty to love, expression, and performance
- **Virgo**: Precision and ritual in service, wellness, and order
- **Libra**: Commitment to harmony, partnership, and aesthetic beauty
- **Scorpio**: Sacred focus on transformation, intimacy, and secrets
- **Sagittarius**: Devotion to truth, freedom, and higher learning
- **Capricorn**: Steady pursuit of purpose, mastery, and legacy
- **Aquarius**: Loyalty to innovation, ideals, and the collective
- **Pisces**: Spiritual dedication to healing, creativity, and compassion

Vesta asks: What fire do you guard at the center of your soul?

She invites you to strip away the noise and return to what is essential — the quiet devotion that fuels your purpose, the sacred ritual that steadies your spirit, the inner flame that no one else sees but you. In a world that pulls you in a thousand directions, Vesta reminds you to tend to your own hearth first — to protect the energy that makes you whole.

**Juno: The Partner**

**Keywords:** Marriage, commitment, equality, soulmate bonds

Juno symbolizes the archetype of committed partnership — the kind that is built to last. Where Venus shows how you love, Juno shows what you need for lasting connection: loyalty, mutual respect, equality, and the ability to grow together through conflict and devotion.

She governs not just who you're drawn to, but what kinds of relational patterns you attract, including your expectations, jealousy, and power dynamics. Juno reveals the type of marriage or soul bond your spirit is wired to seek — and what must be healed to sustain it.

**Mythology:**
Juno, or Hera in Greek myth, was queen of the gods — fiercely devoted to marriage,

despite Zeus's betrayals. She symbolizes both the sanctity of commitment and the challenges that come with it: power dynamics, fidelity, and fairness.

**In Your Chart, Juno Shows:**

- What qualities you seek in a committed partner
- Your patterns around loyalty, jealousy, and power in relationships
- How you approach marriage, equality, and sacred union

**Themes by Sign:**

- **Aries**: Craves passion and equality in autonomy
- **Taurus**: Needs consistency, sensuality, and shared security
- **Gemini**: Seeks mental stimulation and playful intimacy
- **Cancer**: Desires emotional protection and deep roots
- **Leo**: Needs loyalty, admiration, and big-hearted devotion
- **Virgo**: Looks for mutual purpose, care, and thoughtfulness
- **Libra**: Longs for harmony, beauty, and shared values
- **Scorpio**: Needs soulful, honest, all-in commitment
- **Sagittarius**: Craves adventure, learning, and expansion together
- **Capricorn**: Prioritizes devotion, ambition, and mutual endurance
- **Aquarius**: Seeks an unconventional, equal-minded bond
- **Pisces**: Longs for spiritual union and emotional flow

Juno reminds us that love isn't just passion — it's partnership. And true partnership is sacred work.

She speaks to the vows we make, not just with words but with presence: to show up when it's hard, to listen when it's inconvenient, to honor the bond even as we grow and change. Through Juno, we understand that commitment is not the end of freedom — it's where freedom becomes shared purpose. Her wisdom lives in the give and take of real love, where equality isn't just desired — it's required.

**Case Study: A Chiron Awakening**

Let's explore Chiron in real life. **Jordan** has Chiron in **Taurus in the 2nd house**. Growing up, they always felt insecure about money, stability, and self-worth. No matter how much they achieved, it never felt like enough.

In their mid-30s, Jordan lost their job. Instead of spiraling, they began mentoring young entrepreneurs. Over time, they became known not just for their business acumen, but for how they helped others feel worthy of their success. Jordan turned their wound around security into a path of healing for others.

Chiron teaches that your wound isn't a punishment — it's a portal.

### More Case Studies: When Asteroids Speak Loudly

**Ceres in the 4th House: Maya** had Ceres in Cancer in the 4th house — a double dose of maternal energy. She was the rock of her family but constantly put others' needs before her own. When she began therapy in her 40s, she realized that nurturing herself was just as important. She eventually became a grief counselor, helping others navigate familial loss.

**Pallas in the 10th House: Luca** had Pallas in Capricorn in the 10th house. From a young age, he could see systems clearly and had an intuitive grasp of strategy. He became a corporate consultant who specialized in organizational restructuring — spotting patterns, streamlining, and helping others succeed with wisdom and vision.

**Juno in Scorpio in the 8th House: Raya** had Juno here and experienced intense, transformative relationships. She was drawn to partners who forced her to face her shadows. Her biggest growth came through learning the difference between soul-bonding and emotional enmeshment. She later became a therapist who helped couples navigate intimacy and power dynamics.

### Asteroid Interplay with Major Planets

Asteroids don't act in isolation. Their power becomes even clearer when they form aspects with your personal planets.

**Chiron Aspects:**

- **Chiron conjunct Sun**: Deep identity wound. The journey involves embracing self-worth and becoming a mentor.
- **Chiron opposite Moon**: Early emotional trauma may shape your empathy. Great potential for nurturing others.
- **Chiron trine Venus**: Healing through relationships and creativity. Love becomes medicine.

**Ceres Aspects:**

- **Ceres conjunct Moon**: A deeply nurturing soul. May struggle with separation or over-giving.
- **Ceres square Saturn**: Challenges in receiving care. Need to rewrite internal scripts around worthiness.

**Pallas Aspects:**

- **Pallas sextile Mercury**: Strategic thinker. Gifted at pattern recognition and systems-level communication.
- **Pallas conjunct Mars**: Tactical warrior. Knows how to pick the right fight at the right time.

**Vesta Aspects:**

- **Vesta trine Pluto**: Sacred devotion to transformation. Potential for healing and energy work.
- **Vesta opposite Venus**: Tension between sacred focus and romantic needs. Integration needed.

**Juno Aspects:**

- **Juno conjunct Descendant**: Marriage and partnership are core to life lessons.
- **Juno square Uranus**: Attraction to unconventional partners or instability in commitment.

These aspects add depth to your interpretations, giving a voice to subtleties that might otherwise go unnoticed.

### Asteroids in Transit and Progression

Just like planets, asteroids move — and when they **transit** your natal chart or show up in **progressions**, they can trigger major inner developments.

**Chiron Transits:**

When **Chiron transits a natal planet**, old wounds resurface for healing.

- **Chiron conjunct the Sun**: Identity healing, ego restructuring. May feel like an identity crisis — and emerge wiser.
- **Chiron square the Moon**: Family wounds, emotional vulnerability. Can lead to deeper compassion and maternal breakthroughs.

**Ceres Transits:**

Ceres transits highlight nourishment, loss, or emotional nurturing.

- **Ceres conjunct the IC**: Reclaiming home and emotional roots.
- **Ceres opposing Venus**: Conflicts around giving and receiving love. Good time to realign emotional needs.

**Juno Progressions:**

A **progressed Juno** shifting signs or houses might signal a change in your relationship values.

- **Progressed Juno into Libra**: A new emphasis on fairness, harmony, or equal partnership.
- **Progressed Juno into the 7th House**: Major soulmates or marriage energy activated.

These subtle movements can feel like inner nudges — shifts in desire, mission, or values that unfold slowly but profoundly.

### Why Asteroids Matter

While not everyone uses asteroids, they can:

- Clarify unclear areas in your chart

- Add nuance to planetary stories
- Unlock your approach to healing, justice, focus, and love

They don't override planets, but they whisper truths in the spaces between. Asteroids fill in the fine print of your soul contract.

The deeper you go in astrology, the more the "minor" bodies start to speak — and their voices are often the most profound.

# Chapter 14: Lilith, Vertex and Fortune

*Shadow, Fate and Flow*

## Introduction: The Mysterious Forces Behind the Curtain

Astrology doesn't just describe personality or predict timing — it also explores the hidden forces that tug at your soul. In this chapter, we dive into three often-overlooked points that deepen the emotional, karmic, and spiritual dimensions of a birth chart: **Lilith**, the **Vertex axis**, and the **Part of Fortune**.

These points don't correspond to physical planets. Instead, they're symbolic energies — and they reflect the parts of ourselves that are the hardest to name but impossible to ignore. They speak of fate, power, repressed desire, and moments of cosmic flow. They're where the cosmos becomes personal, mystical, and a little bit wild.

If the chart were a novel, Lilith would be the shadowy antihero, the Vertex the chance meeting that changes the plot, and the Part of Fortune the unexpected oasis of ease and joy.

## Dark Moon Lilith: The Untamed Feminine

**Keywords:** Rebellion, sexuality, rage, shadow self, exiled power

**Function in the Chart:** Lilith represents the part of the psyche that refuses to be domesticated. She is where you've swallowed your voice, hidden your truth, or been punished for standing in your power — and she is also where your primal, sovereign self longs to be free. Lilith is raw instinct, creative chaos, sacred rage, and the desire to belong on your own terms.

**Three Faces of Lilith:**

- **Black Moon Lilith:** The lunar apogee — a void-like point that amplifies what's been exiled. Symbolizes where you reclaim your voice, agency, and desire.
- **Asteroid Lilith (1181):** A tangible form of Lilith energy that surfaces through life experiences involving betrayal, estrangement, or emotional sovereignty.

- **Dark Moon Lilith (Waldemath Moon):** A controversial hypothetical point representing psychic and emotional toxins — the shadow of what we suppress. Highly intuitive, often surfacing through dreams and emotional purging.

**Lilith Themes by House:** Each house Lilith falls in speaks to a domain of life where you may have been silenced, judged, or had to fight for ownership of your truth. It also shows where you hold deep power once reclaimed.

**Mythology:** Lilith is not a cautionary tale — she's a reckoning. In Jewish mythology, she was Adam's first wife, created equal. When she refused to submit, she was exiled. This story has turned Lilith into a feminist icon — a mythic figure representing the power of saying "no," of walking away, of embracing the wild.

**In the Birth Chart, Lilith Reflects:**

69. Where you've been deemed "too much" — and how to turn that into power
70. What truths you must reclaim to be whole
71. The kinds of dynamics, desires, and themes that stir deep rage or liberation

**Lilith by Sign (Expanded and Simplified):** These interpretations help you understand how Lilith's wild, rebellious energy expresses itself through each zodiac sign. This energy may be conscious or unconscious, but it often becomes most visible when you feel shamed, suppressed, or fiercely called to reclaim your power.

- **Aries:** You were born to stand up and speak out — Lilith here gives you raw fire and assertive independence. You rebel through boldness and don't like being told what to do.
- **Taurus:** You resist being objectified or controlled materially. Your power lies in sensual self-sufficiency — you reclaim your body, your time, and your values.
- **Gemini:** Words are your weapons and your freedom. Lilith here speaks truth even when it's uncomfortable. You may have been shamed for being "too curious" or "too loud."
- **Cancer:** Your nurturing side has deep edges. You protect fiercely, but may reject traditional gender or family roles. You redefine what emotional safety means on your terms.
- **Leo:** You shine as an act of rebellion. Lilith in Leo doesn't shrink — she demands to be seen and validated, not for fitting in, but for being wholly herself.

- **Virgo:** You reclaim the right to heal, perfect, and serve on your own terms. You may wrestle with shame around sexuality or body image but are empowered through precise discernment.
- **Libra:** You question polite conformity and surface-level harmony. Lilith here reclaims relational power — you're here to love deeply, but not at the cost of your voice or values.
- **Scorpio:** This is Lilith in full shadow queen mode — potent, erotic, transformative. You hold immense power to heal or destroy. You're not afraid of the underworld.
- **Sagittarius:** You challenge moral, cultural, or religious rules. Lilith in Sagittarius is the wild priestess who reclaims freedom through philosophy, humor, and adventure.
- **Capricorn:** You defy being cast as the "obedient climber." Lilith here builds legacy outside the system. You may carry shame around ambition — or learn to wield it with purpose.
- **Aquarius:** Revolutionary and unruly, you defy groupthink. Your rebellion lies in vision — in reshaping society without asking permission.
- **Pisces:** Your emotions and intuition run ocean-deep. Lilith here experiences boundary-blurring and psychic intensity. You reclaim your empathy and sensitivity as superpowers.

Lilith asks: *Where have you been silenced, and what happens when you roar?*
She is not here to be softened or explained away — she is here to be reclaimed. In the birth chart, Lilith is the electric pulse beneath your restraint, the memory of your wildest self before shame took hold. She doesn't seek approval — she seeks liberation. And in freeing her, you reclaim the rawest, most magnetic, and undiluted parts of yourself. Lilith doesn't just stir rebellion — she awakens sacred sovereignty. Wherever she resides in your chart is where you were once subdued — and where you're now prepared to reign.

### The Vertex: Doorways of Fate

**Keywords:** Fated encounters, soul contracts, turning points

**Function in the Chart:** The Vertex is a karmic magnet. It represents the people, events, and moments that shake you awake and steer you off your scripted path into soul territory. Unlike your personal choices (Ascendant), the Vertex operates more like a divine invitation to evolve.

**Vertex vs. Ascendant:** The Ascendant is your conscious interface — how you act and engage with life. The Vertex is your unconscious gateway — where life surprises you, redirects you, or cracks you open. One is a door you open; the other is a door opened for you.

**Vertex in Synastry:** When someone's planet touches your Vertex:

- There's a sense of having "known them forever" — even if you just met.
- Their presence often initiates rapid internal change, even if fleeting.
- These relationships can feel destined, yet also challenging — mirrors of evolution, not comfort.

**Vertex in Transits and Progressions:**

- **Transiting Uranus:** Expect the unexpected — a disruptive but freeing meeting.
- **Transiting Pluto:** A transformation that redefines your trajectory.
- **Progressed Sun/Moon to Vertex:** Major milestones involving identity or relationships.

**Vertex Axis by House (Expanded):**

- **5th/11th:** Romantic and social catalysts that shift creative identity or belonging.
- **6th/12th:** Events that redirect your health, purpose, or connection to the unseen.
- **7th/1st:** Partnerships that alter your self-concept. Major relational karma.
- **8th/2nd:** Resource-sharing, emotional intimacy, or psychological upheaval.
- **9th/3rd:** Teachers, travel, or messages that change your belief system.

**What Is It?** The Vertex is a calculated point (not a planet) found on the western side of the chart. It's sometimes described as a "door to the other side" — the portal through which the soul meets destiny.

**In the Birth Chart, the Vertex Axis Illuminates:**

- What kind of people catalyze growth
- Where you're most receptive to intervention
- The internal lesson carried within outer events

**Vertex by Sign (Expanded):**

- **Aries:** Drawn into action by bold individuals. Your fate is forged through courage.
- **Taurus:** Stability brings fated insight. Material values undergo transformation.
- **Gemini:** Fated messages, ideas, or teachers alter your path.
- **Cancer:** Family or emotional bonds prompt healing and growth.
- **Leo:** Recognition and creative selfhood open new doors.
- **Virgo:** Order and service become transformative vehicles.
- **Libra:** Encounters bring balance and karmic closure.
- **Scorpio:** Fate arrives through depth, merging, and sometimes destruction.
- **Sagittarius:** Beliefs evolve through travel, philosophy, or cultural exchange.
- **Capricorn:** Legacy-shaping figures appear. Ambition is tested and refined.
- **Aquarius:** Radical thinkers shift your worldview.
- **Pisces:** Destiny dissolves boundaries. You're reshaped by the unseen.

The Vertex whispers: *"This isn't just a coincidence. Something bigger is happening."* It is the place where the plot twists — where the script you wrote gets edited by the universe. The Vertex doesn't shout; it pivots you. Often without warning, always with purpose. It arrives through meetings you didn't expect, opportunities you didn't chase, and endings that felt like beginnings in disguise.

This point in your chart doesn't represent what you choose — it reveals what chooses you. And when it activates, something ancient stirs: the memory of agreements made before birth, soul contracts written in stardust. Through the Vertex, you don't just encounter fate — you participate in it.

**The Part of Fortune: The Gold Thread of Joy**

**Keywords:** Prosperity, alignment, flow, success, grace

**What Is It?** The Part of Fortune (or Fortuna) is a sensitive point that shows where you can experience the greatest ease, joy, and natural abundance — not because you chase it, but because you live in alignment with your essence. It is calculated from your Ascendant, Sun, and Moon, making it uniquely tied to your physical, conscious, and emotional layers.

**In the Chart, the Part of Fortune Indicates:**

- The area of life where you feel "in the zone"

- Natural magnetism and fulfillment
- Your potential for meaningful, sustainable success

Unlike Jupiter (which can inflate or exaggerate), the Part of Fortune is subtle. It doesn't promise riches — it reveals where life flows when you're true to yourself.

**Fortune by Sign (Expanded):**

- **Aries:** Fulfillment through fearless leadership, action, and autonomy.
- **Taurus:** Joy in building beauty, enjoying the senses, and honoring consistency.
- **Gemini:** Curiosity leads to abundance. Words are magic. Teach, write, speak.
- **Cancer:** Joy through family, heritage, emotional connection, and care.
- **Leo:** Creativity and visibility open golden paths. Be seen.
- **Virgo:** Fulfillment in mastery, service, and healing work. Integrity is everything.
- **Libra:** Connection, beauty, and diplomacy align you with grace.
- **Scorpio:** Transformation births abundance. Go deep.
- **Sagittarius:** Expansion, wisdom, and authenticity bring good fortune.
- **Capricorn:** Strategic ambition and resilience yield long-term reward.
- **Aquarius:** Innovation and collective purpose unlock unique blessings.
- **Pisces:** Spirituality, imagination, and empathy generate sacred flow.

The Part of Fortune is where effort meets grace — your unique map to abundance through alignment.

But it's more than just success — it's soul-deep contentment. This is not where you strive — it's where you *flow*. It reveals the space in life where you stop fighting the current and begin to swim in rhythm with who you truly are.

Fortuna is the place where you exhale. Where fulfillment feels earned but never forced. When you honor this point, you unlock a path where success feels not just possible, but natural — and joy is no longer a destination, but a state of being.

### When the Chart Whispers

Lilith, the Vertex, and Fortuna don't shout — they *whisper.* They appear in moments of eerie alignment, soul-activating relationships, creative rebellion, or intuitive clarity.

These points don't replace the core structure of your chart — but they reveal layers that are emotional, karmic, and ineffably true. They're the hidden scriptwriters of your story, deepening the drama, plot twists, and grace.

So the next time something feels *too meaningful to be random* — check these three. The stars were likely trying to tell you something all along.

# Chapter 15: Retrogrades and Eclipses

*Cosmic Rewinds and Revelations*

### When the Sky Hits Pause (or Fast-Forwards You into Growth)

Not everything in astrology moves forward — at least not all the time. Some of the most powerful celestial phenomena are not new beginnings or alignments, but **reversals** and **shadows**. Enter: retrogrades and eclipses.

If planets are normally direct, linear narrators, retrogrades are their introspective cousins: less "Go!" and more "Wait, did you miss something?" Meanwhile, eclipses don't ask — they declare. These celestial events turn the volume up on fate, clarity, and change. Together, retrogrades and eclipses signal periods where the cosmos grabs your attention and says: *look again.*

In this chapter, we'll demystify these dramatic and misunderstood sky patterns, explaining what they are, how they work, and what they're really here to teach you.

### Understanding Retrograde Motion

#### What Is a Retrograde?

Retrograde motion is an **optical illusion** — a planet appears to move backward in the sky due to the relative speeds of Earth's orbit. It's like passing another car on the highway: the other car isn't actually moving backward, but from your perspective, it looks that way. In astrology, that apparent reversal carries symbolic weight. **Perception matters** — and when a planet *feels* like it's reversing, it marks a time of reflection, revision, and recalibration.

#### Energetically, Retrogrades Signal:

- A shift from outward to inward
- A need to review, not initiate
- An invitation to retrace steps, reassess motivations, and revise the past
- A slowdown — sometimes welcome, sometimes frustrating

#### The Retrograde Cycle Includes 3 Phases:

72. **Pre-shadow:** The planet slows down — seeds of the issue begin to emerge.
73. **Retrograde:** The official "rewind." Things slow, unravel, or return from the past.
74. **Post-shadow:** The planet resumes direct motion but takes time to regain speed — this is the integration phase.

Retrogrades often feel like walking backward through a room you thought you'd already cleaned. They're not setbacks — they're spiritual audits. They don't cancel growth; they deepen it.

**The Mercury Retrograde Myth (and Truth)**

**Why It Gets a Bad Rap:** Because Mercury rules fast-moving, everyday life — emails, texting, commuting, scheduling — when it retrogrades, we *notice*. It's not that Mercury retrograde causes chaos; it reveals where the cracks are.

**How It Feels:**

- Words come out wrong
- You misunderstand (or get misunderstood)
- Appointments get double-booked
- Old friends or lovers resurface
- You're late for things… or technology betrays you

**Deeper Meaning:** Mercury retrograde is like the universe saying, "Hey, slow down. Don't just *do*, *understand*."

**Mercury Retrograde in Each Element:**

- **Fire Signs (Aries, Leo, Sagittarius):** Rethinking direction, motivation, and impulsivity. Watch for burnout or passionate overreaction.
- **Earth Signs (Taurus, Virgo, Capricorn):** Reevaluating work, routines, money. Productive but may reveal where you've overcommitted.
- **Air Signs (Gemini, Libra, Aquarius):** Miscommunication central. Double-check everything.
- **Water Signs (Cancer, Scorpio, Pisces):** Emotional reprocessing. Dreams, nostalgia, and past wounds resurface.

**Reflection Prompts:**

- What needs revisiting?
- Where have I ignored the details?
- Who or what is returning for a reason?

Mercury retrograde isn't breaking your life — it's giving you a cosmic red pen to edit it better.

**Mercury Retrograde:** 3–4 times a year, for about 3 weeks.

**What Mercury Rules:**

- Communication
- Technology
- Travel
- Thought processes

**The Myth:** Mercury retrograde ruins everything. Your computer will crash, your ex will text, and your vacation will get canceled.

**The Truth:** Mercury retrograde invites you to slow down. It's a cosmic quality-check — helping you catch mistakes, reframe ideas, and reconnect to old insights.

**What to Expect:**

- Miscommunications or emails sent to the wrong person
- Tech issues or travel delays
- Revisiting past conversations, people, or plans

**Best Practices:**

- Avoid signing new contracts unless necessary
- Back up your devices
- Rethink, re-edit, rework, revisit

Think of Mercury retrograde as your brain's software update. It's annoying — but necessary.

**Retrogrades of Other Planets**

Retrogrades of the outer and social planets are longer in duration and occur less frequently, but their impact is no less powerful — especially on collective consciousness, personal maturation, and karmic evolution.

**Venus Retrograde (Every 18 Months, ~40 Days):** Venus governs love, money, aesthetics, and values. When it retrogrades, your heart takes a detour inward.

**What It Does:**

- Reignites past lovers or old wounds in current relationships
- Challenges your self-worth and what you believe you deserve
- Encourages a shift in your relationship to pleasure and beauty

**Themes to Explore:**

- Am I loving from authenticity or fear?
- Do I value myself the way I expect others to?
- What parts of me need to be re-romanced?

**Common Symptoms:** Ghosts of exes, spontaneous makeovers, romantic reassessment, artistic identity shifts

**Mars Retrograde (Every 2 Years, ~60–80 Days):** Mars governs willpower, drive, sex, and how you fight. Its retrograde is like trying to floor the gas pedal with the brakes still on.

**What It Does:**

- Slows physical energy, dampens motivation
- Exposes toxic anger, impulsiveness, or passive aggression
- Rethinks how you pursue goals or express desire

**Reflection Prompts:**

- What am I angry about but not expressing?

- Is my drive fueled by passion or pressure?
- What would it look like to pursue what I want with clarity, not chaos?

**Jupiter Retrograde (Annually, ~4 Months):** This is less a breakdown and more a philosophical sabbatical.

**What It Does:**

- Rethinks belief systems, education paths, travel plans
- Encourages spiritual or intellectual humility
- Internalizes growth: less "go big," more "go inward"

**Reflection Prompts:**

- Have my beliefs become rigid?
- What truths am I learning that require unlearning something old?

**Saturn Retrograde (Annually, ~4.5 Months):** Saturn retrograde is daddy's check-in: Have you learned the lesson yet?

**What It Does:**

- Revisits boundaries, career structures, and long-term goals
- Exposes where discipline has turned into self-denial
- Revises your definition of success, commitment, and responsibility

**Reflection Prompts:**

- What does "maturity" mean to me now?
- Where do I need to step up — or let go?

**Uranus Retrograde (Annually, ~5 Months):** You can't spark revolution outside if you're repressing rebellion inside.

**What It Does:**

- Turns restlessness inward
- Breaks down the inner status quo
- Awakens the parts of you afraid of change — and dares them to shift anyway

**Neptune Retrograde (Annually, ~5–6 Months):** When the fog clears, what do you really see?

**What It Does:**

- Exposes illusions or spiritual bypassing
- Reveals where you've romanticized something toxic
- Invites deep healing and a return to intuitive truth

**Pluto Retrograde (Annually, ~5–6 Months):** When Pluto retrogrades, your shadow starts talking.

**What It Does:**

- Triggers inner transformation and soul excavation
- Brings up buried trauma, control issues, or obsessions
- Forces ego deaths and rebirths — sometimes multiple

These slower retrogrades ask for long-game reflection. They aren't here to ruin your day — they're here to shift your life.

**Venus Retrograde (every 18 months):** Re-evaluates relationships, values, beauty, and money. Exes may reappear. Your relationship with pleasure shifts.

**Mars Retrograde (every 2 years):** Affects motivation, libido, and action. You may feel stuck or reactive. Avoid aggressive confrontations.

**Jupiter Retrograde:** A review of beliefs, education, and personal growth. Opportunity through introspection, not expansion.

**Saturn Retrograde:** Time to reassess boundaries, structures, and long-term goals. What's sustainable? What's cracking?

**Uranus Retrograde:** Rebellion turned inward. Your inner revolutionary wakes up.

**Neptune Retrograde:** Illusions fade. Disillusionment brings clarity. Spiritual fog lifts (and sometimes, the truth stings).

**Pluto Retrograde:** Deep psychological shadow work. You may confront power dynamics, fears, and old emotional patterns.

Retrogrades don't *break* you — they *break open* what's ready for reflection.

### Eclipses: Portals of Cosmic Course Correction

**What Are Eclipses?** Eclipses occur when the Sun, Moon, and Earth align along the Moon's nodes. They come in **pairs** (Solar + Lunar) and occur **every six months**.

#### Types of Eclipses:

- **Solar Eclipse (New Moon):** Begins a fated new chapter
- **Lunar Eclipse (Full Moon):** Ends a karmic cycle or reveals hidden truths

**Astrological Meaning:** Eclipses shake the snow globe. They remove what's stagnant and insert what's fated. Events that occur around eclipses often feel sudden, emotional, and non-negotiable.

#### How to Work With Eclipses:

- Don't manifest or "intend" during an eclipse — just listen.
- Observe what falls away and what arrives unexpectedly.
- Watch for **house placements** and **nodal connections** in your chart.

**Eclipses by Node:**

- **North Node Eclipse:** Opens doors. You may feel a sudden call to your destiny.
- **South Node Eclipse:** A karmic ending or emotional purge. Closure, surrender, or freedom.

Eclipses are the universe's plot twists. Trust the rewrite.

### Dancing with Reversals and Revelations

Retrogrades and eclipses aren't curses — they're **recalibrations**. They create space, strip illusions, and reorient your path. Yes, they can be messy. But they're also magic.

Astrology isn't just about predicting smooth roads. It's about reading the map when the route changes. And these cosmic events are how the universe nudges you — or sometimes yells — to course correct.

When a planet goes retrograde, look within. When an eclipse arrives, look around. When both happen at once… hold your hat, and trust the ride.

# Part V: Practicing Astrology

# Chapter 16: Reading Your Chart

*Making Meaning from Your Map*

## A Tool for Self-Awareness and Insight

Reading your chart isn't about predicting your fate. It's about self-awareness. It's a tool for insight, reflection, and growth — not perfection. You're not trying to become a fortune teller or a walking ephemeris. You're trying to understand why you do what you do, feel what you feel, and crave what you crave.

This chapter is about connecting with your chart on a personal level. It's not about memorizing every asteroid or becoming an expert reader for others — it's about learning to interpret your map with compassion and curiosity. You're not studying astrology to impress anyone else — you're studying to connect more deeply with your own journey.

## What to Keep in Mind When Reading Your Chart

- **You're not looking for rules — you're looking for reflection.** Your chart won't tell you what to do. It will show you how you're wired, what patterns you tend to repeat, and where you're invited to grow.
- **Your chart is a mirror, not a crystal ball.** The goal is insight, not prediction. Use it to deepen your understanding, not box yourself in.
- **Astrology is a conversation.** Let it speak — but also listen to how it lands in your body, your mind, your lived experience.

## Questions to Ask as You Explore

Start with what's real. Don't jump into advanced analysis — begin with honest reflection.

75. "What part of my life feels most active or confusing right now?"
76. "What am I being asked to release, accept, or grow into?"
77. "What themes keep repeating?"
78. "What am I learning about myself lately — and how does my chart speak to that?"

Your birth chart is a layered tool. It can validate your strengths, explain your emotional landscape, and give context to the cycles you're living through. But you get to decide what's meaningful.

### Tips for Reading Your Chart

- **Start with your Big Three:** Your Sun, Moon, and Rising will already give you tons of insight.
- **Look at the houses where you have clusters (stelliums) or big transits.** Those areas are where life is probably loudest.
- **Check the transiting Moon each day.** How does it affect your mood? Start tracking.
- **Journal your reactions to planetary movements.** You don't need to analyze everything — just notice how you feel.
- **Be kind to yourself.** If a placement or aspect seems "hard," don't spiral. Every chart has tension — that's how we grow.

### How to Stay Grounded While You Explore

It's easy to go down the rabbit hole and start seeing every retrograde or Pluto square as a looming crisis. Don't. Astrology should feel like a soft light — not a spotlight interrogating your every move.

- Use it as a way to get curious, not to self-diagnose.
- Don't jump to conclusions about relationships, jobs, or your future based on one placement.
- If something stirs emotion, take a break. Go outside. Breathe. Then come back when you feel ready.

### You're the Reader and the Story

There's power in looking up at the sky and saying, "What's the lesson here?" There's even more power in listening to your own answer.

So read your chart — not to find out who you are, but to remember who you've always been.

The stars aren't telling you what to do. They're whispering: "*This is your story. Want to read the next page?*"

# Chapter 17: Living Your Astrology

*Daily Integration, Reflection, and Rhythms*

### Living Your Astrology Day to Day

Astrology isn't just something you learn — it's something you live. Once you understand your chart, the real transformation begins when you observe it in action, day after day, through the subtle and not-so-subtle shifts of life. This chapter will help you translate what you've learned into a lived practice, using your chart as a compass for emotional self-awareness, timing, and growth.

Whether you're using astrology to navigate career decisions, emotional ups and downs, or relationship patterns, this practice becomes more powerful the more you engage with it. And the best part? You don't need to memorize ephemerides or know every asteroid. You just need to stay curious and make space for reflection.

This chapter is about making astrology part of your everyday self-reflection. It's about engaging with the energies of the sky in a way that's meaningful, intuitive, and accessible — no advanced training required. Whether you're journaling through a Saturn transit, noticing emotional shifts during a Full Moon, or reflecting on a recurring pattern in your chart, this chapter will help you connect astrology to real life — gently and personally.

Let's explore how to bring your chart to life through observation, reflection, and daily practice.

### What to Look for in Chart Support Tools

You don't need high-tech gadgets or pricey subscriptions. What matters most is having access to clear, intuitive tools that help you observe what's happening in the sky in relation to your chart. Whether you're using a simple printable wheel or a digital chart generator, look for tools that help you:

- Generate natal, progressed, transit, and relationship charts
- Choose between house systems (Placidus, Whole Sign, Equal, etc.)
- Customize aspects and include optional points like Chiron, Lilith, or the Vertex
- Offer clarity and intuitive visuals

- Provide interpretive support that's informative rather than overly vague

If you're ever unsure which tools to try, look for ones that:

79. Are actively maintained and updated
80. Allow you to export your chart and notes
81. Are praised by other astrology students for clarity and ease

Tip: Focus less on finding the “perfect” tool, and more on choosing one you'll actually use. Consistency is more magical than complexity.

### Tracking the Moon: Your First Cosmic Companion

The Moon changes signs every 2.5 days and governs emotions, instincts, and rhythms. Tracking the Moon is one of the most accessible and insightful ways to tune into astrology.

**Try This:**

- Notice how your mood shifts with each Moon sign.
- Journal how Full Moons and New Moons feel for you.
- Track your own Moon sign in transits — when the Moon returns to your natal Moon, note your emotional weather.

Over time, you'll see patterns. Maybe you're extra productive during Aries Moons or nostalgic under Cancer Moons. The Moon teaches you how to ride your emotional tides.

### Noting Transits and Patterns

Transits are where astrology gets dynamic. They reveal how current planetary movements activate your natal chart. You don't need to track every minor transit — just the ones that really move you.

**Focus on:**

- **Saturn, Uranus, Neptune, and Pluto**: Long-term change, growth, challenge, evolution
- **Jupiter transits**: Expansion, luck, and opportunity
- **Venus and Mars**: Short-term passion, romance, drive
- **Mercury retrogrades**: Times to review, reflect, rework

**Daily Practice:**

- Pick one or two planets to track each month.
- Reflect: What's coming up emotionally, mentally, spiritually?
- Compare current transits to times in the past when those planets made similar moves.

Patterns emerge. And astrology becomes less about prediction and more about partnership.

### Keeping a Cosmic Journal

Astrology only gets richer with personal experience. Keeping a cosmic journal grounds the language of the stars in your real life.

**Ideas for Journaling:**

- Log what the Moon is doing and how you feel
- Track major transits to your chart and note themes
- Reflect on questions like:
    - What energy is most active in my chart right now?
    - What am I being asked to grow into?
    - Which parts of myself are evolving?

**Why It Helps:**

- You build a personal astrology archive
- You catch patterns more easily
- You connect astrology to your intuition

Over time, your journal becomes a storybook — not just of your life, but of your evolution. You'll start to see not just what the stars are doing, but how you're dancing with them.

### Final Thoughts: Let the Stars Be Your Companion

Astrology isn't just a system of meaning — it's a conversation. And that conversation becomes richer when you respond.

Let your practice be simple, sincere, and soul-driven. You're not doing this to become an expert — you're doing this to become more *you.*

Notice the sky. Feel the transits. Reflect when the Moon feels full in your chest. Listen when Saturn whispers a lesson or when Neptune blurs your dreams into art. This is how the stars speak. Not always in logic — but always in meaning.

You now carry the language of the cosmos. Use it gently. Use it wisely. Use it with wonder.

You're not just reading the stars anymore.

***You're becoming one.***

# Appendix

## Glossary of Terms

Below is an expanded glossary of key astrology terms — from the foundational to the more advanced — organized alphabetically to support your ongoing understanding and exploration.

**Anaretic Degree:** The final degree of any sign (29°), often representing a point of crisis, urgency, or mastery.

**Angular Houses:** The 1st, 4th, 7th, and 10th houses. These houses are tied to major life themes: self, home, relationships, and career.

**Aspect:** The angle formed between two planets. Aspects describe how different parts of your personality interact. Major aspects include conjunction, sextile, square, trine, and opposition.

**Arabic Parts (Lots):** Calculated points in the chart that blend planetary influences. The most famous is the Part of Fortune, but others include the Part of Spirit, Part of Love, and Part of Death.

**Ascendant (Rising Sign):** The sign rising on the eastern horizon at your time of birth. It represents how others perceive you and how you begin new experiences.

**Asteroids:** Small celestial bodies like Ceres, Pallas, Juno, Vesta, and Chiron, which add nuance to themes around healing, devotion, partnership, and creative power.

**Cadent Houses:** The 3rd, 6th, 9th, and 12th houses. These relate to processing, transition, and internalization.

**Chart Ruler:** The planetary ruler of your Ascendant sign. This planet gives insight into your life's direction and dominant themes.

**Chart Shape:** The overall distribution of planets across the natal chart. Common types include Bowl, Bucket, Splash, Bundle, and Locomotive — each suggesting a different psychological orientation.

**Chiron:** An asteroid that represents our deepest wound and potential for healing and wisdom. Often called the "Wounded Healer."

**Composite Chart:** A single chart created from the midpoints of two natal charts. Used to explore the dynamics of a relationship.

**Conjunction:** An aspect where two planets are close together, blending energies. Can intensify both harmonious and difficult traits.

**Cusp:** The transitional point between two zodiac signs. A person born near a cusp may show traits of both signs but is still defined by the exact sign the Sun was in at their birth.

**Day Chart (Diurnal):** A chart with the Sun above the horizon (houses 7–12), often indicating a more outwardly focused personality.

**Decan:** A subdivision of each zodiac sign into three ten-degree segments, each ruled by a different planetary influence, adding nuance to how a sign is expressed.

**Decumbiture Chart:** A chart cast for the onset of illness, used in medical astrology to diagnose and forecast outcomes.

**Descendant:** The sign on the cusp of the 7th house. It represents how you relate to others and what you seek in partnerships.

**Dignity and Debility:** Terms used to describe how strong or challenged a planet is based on its sign placement. Includes rulership, exaltation, detriment, and fall.

**Dispositor:** The planet that rules the sign another planet is in. Dispositors help trace energetic loops and dominant themes in the chart.

**Dispositor Chain:** A sequence showing how planets are linked by rulership, helping identify the final dispositor (planet at the end of the chain), which can act as a key influence.

**Dominant Planet:** A planet that stands out due to aspects, placement, or angularity. It plays a lead role in the personality.

**Electional Astrology:** The practice of choosing the most astrologically favorable time to begin an event, such as a wedding, launch, or travel.

**Elements:** The four classical elements — Fire, Earth, Air, and Water — represent essential energetic styles. Fire (Aries, Leo, Sagittarius) is passionate and dynamic; Earth (Taurus, Virgo, Capricorn) is grounded and practical; Air (Gemini, Libra, Aquarius) is intellectual and communicative; Water (Cancer, Scorpio, Pisces) is emotional and intuitive.

**Ephemeris:** A reference table showing the daily positions of the planets for specific dates.

**Essential Dignities:** A traditional system measuring a planet's strength based on sign, degree, and position. Often used in classical astrology.

**Fixed Stars:** Ancient stellar points with mythological and predictive meaning, used for deeper interpretation beyond planets.

**Fixed Signs:** Taurus, Leo, Scorpio, Aquarius. These signs are stabilizers, focused, and tend to resist change.

**Grand Cross:** A challenging pattern formed when four planets square each other and oppose across the chart, creating dynamic tension.

**Heliocentric Astrology:** A system of astrology that uses the Sun — rather than the Earth — as the center of the solar system for calculations.

**Hemisphere Emphasis:** Interpreting a chart based on planetary concentration in the upper (public) vs. lower (private), or left (self-initiated) vs. right (other-oriented) halves.

**Horary Astrology:** A system of answering specific questions based on the chart cast for the moment the question is asked.

**House:** One of the 12 divisions of the natal chart, each representing a different area of life (e.g., work, family, self-expression).

**IC (Imum Coeli):** The lowest point of the chart, found at the cusp of the 4th house. It represents your roots, home life, and inner world.

**Interception:** When a sign is entirely contained within a house and doesn't appear on any house cusp. Indicates a potential area of suppressed or delayed expression.

**Lilith (Black Moon Lilith):** A sensitive point associated with raw feminine power, sexual autonomy, rejection, and shadow work.

**Lunar Return:** A chart cast for the moment the Moon returns to its natal position each month. Offers insight into emotional themes for the coming weeks.

**Midheaven (MC):** The highest point in the chart, on the cusp of the 10th house. Symbolizes career, public life, and legacy.

**Midpoint:** The halfway point between two planets or chart points. Often used in relationship and psychological astrology for nuanced interpretation.

**Modalities:** Cardinal (initiators), Fixed (sustainers), and Mutable (adapters) are the three modalities that express how each sign takes action.

**Mutable Signs:** Gemini, Virgo, Sagittarius, Pisces. These signs are adaptable, flexible, and oriented toward change.

**Natal Chart:** A map of the sky at the exact time and location of your birth, showing planetary positions in signs and houses.

**Nodes (North & South):** Points where the Moon's orbit intersects the ecliptic. North Node represents soul growth; South Node represents past life comfort zones.

**Nocturnal Chart:** A chart with the Sun below the horizon (houses 1–6), indicating a more inwardly focused nature.

**Opposition:** An aspect formed when two planets are 180 degrees apart. Creates polarity, contrast, and the need for balance.

**Orbs:** The range of degrees within which an aspect is considered active. A tight orb means stronger influence.

**Out-of-Bounds Planet:** A planet that travels beyond the Sun's maximum declination, often indicating extreme or unconventional expression of that planet's traits.

**Parans:** In fixed star astrology, the relationship between a star and a planet as they rise, culminate, or set simultaneously — often used for personal destiny themes.

**Part of Fortune (Fortuna):** A calculated point representing joy, prosperity, and natural talents when the Sun, Moon, and Ascendant are in balance.

**Planetary Hours:** An ancient system of dividing the day into segments ruled by different planets. Used in magical or timing practices.

**Planetary Sect:** A traditional concept that evaluates a planet's strength depending on whether it is in a day or night chart.

**Precession:** The slow movement of the Earth's rotational axis, which causes a shift in the apparent position of the constellations over time. A key concept in sidereal vs. tropical astrology debates.

**Progression (Secondary):** A symbolic predictive technique where one day of life after birth equals one year of life. Tracks inner evolution.

**Quincunx (Inconjunct):** A 150-degree aspect that represents tension and the need for adjustment between two incompatible energies.

**Retrograde:** When a planet appears to move backward in the sky. Symbolizes review, revision, and inward focus.

**Retrograde Loop:** The full apparent motion of a planet as it moves forward, retrogrades, and then moves forward again — used for mapping extended planetary influence.

**Retrograde Shadow:** The degrees a retrograde planet will pass over before and after its actual retrograde motion. The pre-shadow and post-shadow periods offer context to the full retrograde cycle.

**Sabian Symbols:** A set of symbolic images assigned to each of the 360 degrees of the zodiac, used for spiritual or intuitive interpretation.

**Sect:** A classification in traditional astrology that distinguishes planets in day (diurnal) and night (nocturnal) charts.

**Sextile:** A harmonious 60-degree aspect. Encourages opportunity, support, and cooperation between planets.

**Solar Arc:** A predictive technique where all planets in the chart are moved forward at the same rate as the progressed Sun. Used to time major life events.

**Solar Return:** A chart cast for the moment the Sun returns to its exact position from birth. Used for annual forecasting.

**Square:** A tense 90-degree aspect. Represents friction, challenge, and growth through conflict.

**Stellium:** A grouping of three or more planets in the same sign or house. Indicates concentrated energy and emphasis in that area.

**Succedent Houses:** The 2nd, 5th, 8th, and 11th houses. These follow the angular houses and deal with stabilization and support.

**Sun Sign:** The zodiac sign the Sun was in at your birth. Represents your core essence, ego, and identity.

**Synastry:** The comparison of two natal charts to assess relationship compatibility.

**Transit:** The current movement of planets as they interact with your natal placements. Transits show temporary themes and life events.

**Trine:** A flowing 120-degree aspect. Symbolizes natural talent, harmony, and ease.

**Unaspected Planet:** A planet with no major aspects to other planets in the chart. It often functions in an exaggerated or independent way.

**Vertex:** A sensitive point on the chart often tied to fate, destiny, and significant encounters.

**Void of Course Moon:** A period when the Moon makes no applying aspects before changing signs. Traditionally seen as a time when actions may lack follow-through or direction.

**Yod (Finger of God):** A rare aspect pattern involving two planets in sextile both quincunx to a third. Indicates karmic adjustment and spiritual purpose.

**Zodiac Signs:** The twelve signs of the zodiac (Aries through Pisces) represent twelve archetypal energies. Each sign expresses unique traits, modes of behavior, and ways of engaging with the world.

# A Note from the Author

If *Astrology 101: The Language of the Stars* offered you clarity, curiosity, or a deeper sense of connection, I'd be truly grateful if you shared your thoughts in a review.

Just a few words can help others discover the book and support future creations in this series.

You can leave a review here:
**www.amazon.com/review/create-review?asin=B0F59BNLDM**

Thank you for being part of this journey.

With appreciation,
**Isla Quinn**

Printed in Great Britain
by Amazon

61774186R00092